SINGAPORE IN 12 DISHES

HOW TO EAT LIKE YOU LIVE THERE

redporkpress

THE SUPER TREE
GROVE AT GARDENS
BY THE BAY

CONTENTS

ABOUT
SINGAPORE

Lying at the very **tip of the Malay Peninsula**, the city state of **Singapore is a cosmopolitan hub**. A centre of commerce, transport and finance, it draws international high-flyers after a slice of the good life ... and plenty of visitors. Only a sovereign nation since 1965 (it was part of Malaysia after achieving **independence from Britain in 1963**, but that didn't last long), it has one of the world's highest GDP per capita. It was in 1819 that Sir Stamford Raffles instigated the vigorous **free-trade policy that lies at the heart of its economic success** – that and the hard work and ingenuity of the inhabitants. With no significant natural resources, Singapore's wealth is based squarely on trade and commerce – the port here is one of the busiest in the world.

First-time visitors are inevitably struck by Singapore's **orderly beauty**, **clean greenness**, **efficient infrastructure** and the sense of safety. Everything here works, and works well. The old co-exists with the new and the East is as visible as the West. Its population of just over 5.8 million live, for the most part, in high-rise apartments, and comprises **a fascinating ethnic mix** – another of Singapore's selling points. Malays (around 13%), Chinese (about 74%) and Indians (approximately 9%) are the largest groups and their blend of dress, religion, language, festivals and foods are reflected in Singapore's **dynamic multi-culturalism**. The total land area of the country is just 719 square kilometres and, while the place is busy, it never feels sardine-like (with the possible exception of Orchard Road's malls and the metro stations at rush hour). With **plenty of parks, gardens, riverside walkways** and other restful areas, you're never too far from a lush, peaceful pocket, when the urban action gets too much.

The core of downtown Singapore wraps around the **old colonial district**, taking in the banks of the Singapore River. This is where you'll find some lovely old landmark buildings, plenty of five-star hotels, corporate HQs, national museums, galleries and iconic sights. Such as the **stunning Gardens By The Bay**, built on reclaimed land, the ▷

Raffles and Fullerton hotels, the Art Science Museum, the Singapore Flyer and the quirky, 70-tonne, **8.6-metre tall Merlion statue** spouting water into Marina Bay. Half fish and half lion (yes, really), it's become the **mythical symbol of the city**. The fish part (the body) represents Singapore's origins as a fishing village called Temasek, which in Javanese means 'sea town'. The lion part (its head) references Singapore's other name, **Singapura, literally 'lion city'**. BTW, no lions ever did inhabit Singapore; tigers were a more likely scenario.

The various enclaves near the CBD have their own, distinct character. Clamorous **Chinatown, with its tea shops, goldsmiths, old shophouses**, Pagoda Street market, ornate temples, dim sum eateries, barbecue meat shops, hidden alleys and general bustle, is a slice of Chinese life. **Little India** (see pg 79) is one of the **earthier parts of town**; affordable accommodation and eateries serving delicious Indian fare make it a good base for **travellers on a budget**. Or just those yearning for a bit of grit and an edge. Kampong Glam (see pg 80) is **Malay and Arab in flavour** and dominated by the gorgeous Sultan mosque. Here you find hip Haji Lane, with its groovy little boutiques, bars and cafes. **Orchard Road is world-famed** for shiny malls, luxury brands and consumerism on a gobsmacking scale. It's also home to some great hotels and top-notch restaurants. Beyond these areas, there's **Geylang**, an excellent place for some authentic vibes; the old-world shops and eateries service locals, not tourists. **Katong** and **Joo Chiat** in the East, are lovely. Originally, they were home to wealthy Peranakans (see pg 102) who built **ornate mansions and terraced houses**, some of which you still see today. There's excellent dining to be had around here – everything from a casual bowl of *laksa* to mod-Asian share plates in upscale surrounds.

Singapore, often nicknamed 'Singabore', has worked hard to throw off a certain reputation for being bland, overly manicured and fun-free. Its future vision is bound up in **sustainability, eco-diversity and becoming a city literally built in a garden**, and it's well on the way to being that. Greater Singapore is home to **world-class sights** such as the Singapore Zoo, the Jurong Bird Park, Sentosa Island (great for families) and the Botanic Gardens, with their breathtaking orchid displays. Trees and tropical plants are literally everywhere in the city ▷

At Kwong Satay (see pg 101)

On Orchard Road

On Geylang Road, in Geylang

Dim sum at Majestic Bay Seafood Restaurant (see pg 61, 91)

INTERIOR OF
MICHELIN-STARRED
CANDLENUT
(see pg 109)

– even growing out of hotels (check out the Park Royal on Pickering, for example) and down the sides of highways. **Fort Canning is an expansive, beautiful and central green lung**, popular with joggers and strollers. As are the Singapore River and Marina Bay areas.

GETTING AROUND SINGAPORE IS SIMPLE – the **MRT (train) network is extensive, speedy** and also extremely cheap. English signage and English-speaking inhabitants **make self navigation a cinch**. The **weather is hot and humid year round**, with May to September the hottest period, **January the coolest** and November the wettest. Visitor numbers are consistently pretty high, with a relative lull in August to October, although September when the Grand Prix is on is the exception. Basically, it's always busy with plenty going on.

Random fun facts

+ You can get a hefty fine for not flushing a toilet in Singapore after using it
+ AND ... elevators are fitted with urine-detection devices which set off alarms and summon the police when activated. Just ... don't
+ The Bukit Timah Nature Reserve in the north of Singapore contains more tree species than does the whole of North America
+ There are actually 63 islands in Singapore, some uninhabited or used by the military
+ Buildings here aren't allowed to go over 280 metres, partly on account of the heavy air traffic
+ Singapore currently is rated the fifth least corrupt country on earth
+ Singaporeans are officially the fastest walking pedestrians in the world, strutting at a rate of 6.15km per hour on average
+ Chewing gum is only legal with a medical prescription
+ The five stars on the national flag signify democracy, peace, progress, justice and equality
+ Singapore currently has the highest concentration of millionaires in the world
+ Singapore's diversity has given rise to Singlish, a colloquial, local form of English
+ Singapore, Monaco and Vatican City are the world's only remaining city states

At Thian Hock Keng Temple

Orchids, Botanic Gardens

Doorman at Raffles Hotel

Designer stores on Orchard Road

The Merlion in action

THE ICONIC HOTEL
MARINA BAY SANDS

ABOUT SINGAPORE FOOD

Singapore is **a nation of food obsessives** and eating, it's fair to say, is a national pastime. If people aren't currently eating, they're talking about eating and when they do eat, they're photographing, appraising and then posting opinions online about what they've just consumed. And fair enough too; **the food is amazing**. And there's no shortage of outlets – it's estimated there are **more than 6500 eating establishments** in the city, with an average of two new ones opening daily (according to the Accounting and Corporate Regulatory Authority).

Every cuisine in the world is represented among Singapore's fine diners, bistros, canteens and cafes and much of it is extremely good indeed. International chefs of the Joël Robuchon and Tetsuya Wakuda calibre run kitchens here, and **Michelin guide accolades twinkle and shine**. But the **local food, considered a tourist attraction in its own right**, deserves your focus on a short trip. It's diverse, spawned over centuries and carrying the **threads of the various immigrant populations** who have intersected here. Malay, Chinese, Indian, Peranakan (see pg 102), Indonesian and British influences abound. No matter the budget, even if yours is tight, there's incredible food to be had.

Loosely (very loosely), Singaporean food can be divided into meat, seafood, rice, noodle, sweet and snack dishes. Some local communities adhere to strict dietary restrictions (**vegetarian Hindus and halal Muslims** primarily), which adds another layer to the food selection. Popular breakfasts include toast, butter and *kaya*, a jam made from coconut, eggs, sugar and pandan leaves. Commonly served with half-boiled eggs, it's de rigueur to wash the whole lot down with *kopi* (see pg 24), the addictive local coffee brew, which is softened with lashings of condensed milk. Congee, steamed Chinese-style buns, *chee cheong fun* (glutinous rice roll), *chwee kueh* (steamed rice-flour cakes topped with pickled radish and chilli paste) *roti prata* (see pg 18), *appom* (a Southern Indian pancake made with ▷

Nasi lemak (see pg 34)

In Chinatown

Thian Hock Keng Temple

Park Royal on Pickering

Ang ku kueh (see pg 118)

13

EATING LUNCH AT
OLD AIRPORT ROAD
FOOD CENTRE
(see pg 52)

fermented rice-flour batter and served with coconut milk and sugar) and *nasi lemak* (see pg 34) are typical choices.

Many of Singapore's eateries are in hawker centres (see pg 38), where locals frequently take their meals. **Hawker food is incredibly cheap and choices are vast.** Centres are generally open-sided, standalone buildings filled with individual vendors who operate out of small kitchens – the size of hawker centres varies but most are pretty big, with **dozens of dishes on offer.** You find them near transport hubs and housing estates and without great difficulty – they are everywhere. Shopping malls all have excellent food courts, which are essentially hawker centres with aircon and artificial lighting. Because of their location, they tend to be marginally more expensive than the hawker alternative.

Chinese food in Singapore is predominantly southern Chinese, with **Cantonese** (known for its gentle flavours and great finesse), **Hokkien** (*Hokkien mee* or 'fried noodles' and *bak kut teh* are two classic dishes) and **Teochew** (famed for seafood and vegetarian dishes and for its overall delicacy) the main styles. Not only well represented among hawker eateries, there are squillions of restaurants dedicated to Chinese food too. These run the gamut of fine dining, smart-casual, mod-Chinese and earthy *zi char* places; *zi char* is a Hokkien term describing establishments serving home-style meals. Prices in such places are wallet friendly, the vibe's informal and portions are generous, making *zi char* popular with groups and families.

Indian fare is concentrated in Little India (see pg 79), a name for this area concocted by the Tourism Board in the 1980s. It's changing a little, luring a few cafes and boutique breweries – but it doesn't look in danger of being anything other than **overwhelmingly subcontinental** any time soon. The area around Sri Veeramakaliamman Temple holds clusters of Tamil restaurants – think *dosa* and myriad vegetarian dishes, like *paruppu urundai kuzhambu*, or lentil dumplings in tamarind curry. Along Racecourse Road and Serangoon Road, near the Little India MRT, you'll find more Northern and other regionally focused places, with their *tandoor* and *biryani* offerings. At the northern end of Little India, around the famed Mustafa Centre, there's some excellent halal food and home-cooking places. The dining options in Little India could easily keep you busy for a week, with street-side sights and smells that are compelling too.

Malay fare, which can overlap with Indonesian (notably Sumatran and Javanese), can be found everywhere. After all, **Singapore is,** ▷

geographically, Malaysian. Dry spices, tamarind, *belacan* (fermented shrimp paste), aromatics like lime leaves and lemongrass and coconut milk are common ingredients. Chinese elements such as fried tofu puffs have been integrated too, **giving Singaporean-Malay food a unique spin**. *Nasi padang*, or white rice served with a variety of curries and other sides, is a typical dish. *Nasi ambeng* is similar but comprises larger plates and more accompaniments, suited to group sharing. Various noodle dishes, *laksa, nasi lemak* (see pgs 30, 34), a whole raft of curried and fried foods, **the iconic *satay, rendang*, barbecued stingray and *otah otah***, a spicy fish paste grilled in banana leaves, are representative. The entire repertoire is vast.

Then there are cross-cultural dishes – *satay bee hoon* (rice noodles with squid, beancurd puffs, water spinach and cockles in satay sauce), fish head curry (see pg 72), cereal prawns (prawns fried in a sweet cereal coating) and *rojak* (see pg 51), for example. **And salted egg anything.** Salted egg yolk, literally the finely grated yolk of salted egg, has a rich and unique flavour, is all the rage and seems to flavour everything. There are salted egg macarons, peach and salted egg tarts, steamed salted egg dumplings, salted egg ice-cream, fried salted egg prawns, salted egg chicken wings and salted egg crab. Just for starters. You'll also encounter salted egg with, in and on pasta, pizza, fried onion rings and doughnuts. Warn your cardiologist.

Singapore is a fantastic place for eating seafood – chilli and black pepper crab are among the most iconic dishes. Singaporeans are some of the biggest consumers of seafood in Asia and they'll pay a lot for it – a seafood meal tends to be expensive. Crabs from Sri Lanka, salmon from Canada, oysters from France and lobster from Maine are just some of the critters you'll find on menus and buffets. It's worth mentioning that, as it **doesn't produce or harvest much of its own food supply** (land and fishing grounds are very limited), 90% of food is imported from elsewhere. Malaysia, China and Australia are the main sources of imported vegetables, for example, and Malaysia, China and the US, the top sources of fruit. **The quality of raw materials tends to be high**, in keeping with local discernment – it's unlikely you'll ever have bad food in Singapore. **Note that there is no tipping culture as a service charge (10%), as well as GST (7%) and Government tax (1%), are added** at point of sale – these are also known as the dreaded 'plus plus'. So keep those in mind when you survey menus – the taxes aren't added until you pay at the end and if you've not factored them in, the wash-up can come as a surprise. ◆

Salted egg lobster

Steamed cakes called huat kueh

Katong *laksa* (see pg 33)

Buddha Tooth Relic Temple in Chinatown

FRIED OYSTER OMELETTE

虫豪煎

A TYPICAL SERVE
OF *ROTI PRATA*
AND GRAVY

Crisp and oily (outside), chewy (inside) and terribly moreish (every damned bit), eating *prata* is one of the best ways to start your Singapore day. Either plain or filled with egg, cheese, onion or even banana, it's the fried flatbread of your wildest dreams.

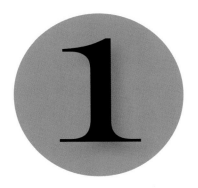

ROTI PRATA

Done right, that is. And locals do grumble about quality diving over the years. Factory-made dough is often (though not always) used, instead of being fashioned by hand as it once always was. Many cooks use inferior margarine, not ghee, for cooking. In the old days, immigrant cooks eager to get ahead sank or swam on the quality of their *roti*; now, lots of hired hands with no personal stake in the reputation of a place aren't so spurred. But, hey – unless you're an aficionado, the nuances of *prata* perfection might well flip right over your head. There are still plenty of great places to get your *roti* on.

The same as *roti canai* (the Malaysian name), *roti prata* originated in southern India and is mostly associated with Chennai; in Hindi, *roti* means 'bread' and *prata* means 'flat'. Indian migrants introduced the dish to Singapore and it's long been a fixture. It's made from a simple, ▷

ROTI PRATA

unleavened wheat flour dough that's kneaded until shiny and very smooth. Divided into serving-sized portions, each piece of dough is rolled, stretched and flipped into a large, thin sheet to order, then smeared lightly with ghee (or margarine). After that, it's subject to a series of deft folds and flips, spun in the air and thrown against an oiled work surface numerous times. These manoeuvres require great skill, creating the many layers required for the proper light, flaky texture of the cooked bread. It's not the sort of thing people attempt to make at home.

Salted egg *prata* at Spring Leaf

Shaped then cooked to order, *roti* should be eaten when still hot or they lose their allure, becoming heavy and dull tasting. It's worth noting there are slightly different styles depending on the vendor – some are crunchier, and others are denser and heavier. *Roti* are served with curry (fish, mutton or chicken), *dhal* (spiced lentils), *sambal* or a selection of these – the idea is, you rip bits of hot bread apart with your hands, dip them in the curry, then scoff. Order two or three, depending on hunger levels – one *roti* won't really scratch the surface.

Roti tisu, Mahamoodiya

Aside from the previously listed variations, *prata* can also be flavoured with condensed milk, honey, garlic, mushroom, chicken floss, chocolate, fruits, peanut butter and even ice-cream and durian, turning it into more of a dessert than breakfast. ◆

Folding egg inside a *roti* before frying

Roti plaster

A stack of cooked *roti*

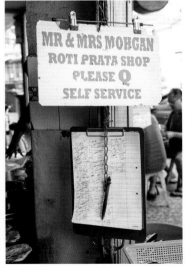
MR & MRS MOHGAN
ROTI PRATA SHOP
PLEASE Q
SELF SERVICE

Some *roti* variations

Roti plaster:
an egg roti but, instead of cooking the egg inside the flatbread, as is usual, it's fried into the exterior.

Prata bomb:
a thicker version of prata, made by coiling the dough into a round. It has more layers, making it softer, and inside are lashings of margarine and sugar, kaya (coconut jam), honey or cheese.

Tissue prata (or roti tisu):
an ultra-thin, crisp prata that comes as a towering cone. When cooked with sugar, it's caramelised and sweetish.

Coin prata:
as the name suggest, these are small prata, and they're fatter and crisper than the regular sort. You get five or six per serve.

Roti john:
nothing like roti prata, this Singaporean invention probably dates from the 1960s. It comprises meat, egg and onion cooked in a pan, with split, fluffy bread rolls pressed into the top. Once the egg mix is firm, the whole thing is flipped so the bread can toast. Served with chilli sauce and mayo and cut into pieces.

Murtabak:
this hefty fried flatbread uses a similar dough and stretching/flipping technique. It's filled with a variety of things — meat/fish (mutton, sardine or chicken) or vegetables like cabbage or onion, the filling held together by egg. The mix is strengthened by a layer of cooked roti dough, which goes on the stretched uncooked dough, before it's filled and folded.

ROTI WITH HAM, EGG AND CHEESE AT SPRING LEAF

WHERE TO EAT

MR & MRS MOHGAN'S SUPER CRISPY ROTI PRATA
7 Crane Road, Joo Chiat.
6.30am-1.30pm (closed Tues and Wed on the 3rd week of the month)
This place, in an old *kopi tiam* in Joo Chiat and down a pleasantly quiet street, is often mooted when conversation turns to deciding on the best *roti* in Singapore. For more than 30 years they've been making their own *roti* from scratch and, as the name suggests, they're very crisp. There are three sides to choose from – *dhal*, fish curry or mutton curry. It's a frenzy here on a weekend morning, such is their popularity. So if you come then, expect to queue.

ALWADI
970 Geylang Road.
24 hours, daily
Geylang Serai, a residential precinct, is a top place to both find authentic Malay and Indian Muslim fare and to rub shoulders with locals. A food court in the ground floor of the Tristar complex, Alwadi is always bustling and presents some excellent dining options, including freshly cooked *murtabak*, *roti prata* and *roti john*.

SPRING LEAF PRATA PLACE
57b Jalan Tua Kong.
7am-12am, daily
Seized by a *prata* urge on your way to Changi Airport? Fly off the main ECP and pull in here – satisfaction guaranteed. A mod-suburban Indian eatery with a few branches, they don't half do imaginative things with *prata* and *murtabak* – the salted egg and prawn *prata*, oozing with rich goodness and not a few curry leaves, is a case in point.

CASUARINA CURRY RESTAURANT
187 Macpherson Road.
10am-12am Mon-Fri, 7am-12am Sat-Sun
They've won awards, they've been around since 1992 and they even run *roti*-making workshops, if you want to learn to DIY. There's much to love about Casuarina, with their 40-odd types of *roti*, including mushroom-cheese, sausage-cheese, banana and chocolate. There are a few branches – this one is near Geylang. The original is at 136 Upper Casuarina Road, off Upper Thomson.

SIN MING ROTI PRATA
#01-51 Jin Fa Kopitiam, 24 Sin Ming Road.
6am-7pm, daily
Another contender for the town's best *roti*. Their handmade breads are crunchy on the outside, chewy and fluffy on the inside and full of good, buttery flavour.

The curries have their fans too, with their deep, spicy flavours and hefty gravies. Highly recommended.

MAHAMOODIYA
335 Bedok Road.
24 hours, daily
They achieve their signature crispness by cooking the *prata* in a literal pool of hot oil – look away if you're fat phobic. But ... that crunch; it's sublime. The best thing about venturing out to Bedok to eat here is the vibe, which is chilled. Very. It's almost like dining in a village, especially in their lean-to section.

ZAM ZAM RESTAURANT
679-699 North Bridge Road.
8am-11pm, daily
Since 1908, they've been the *murtabak* kings of Singapore – this is THE place to get your fill of this crazy-good filled flat bread. Positioned on a corner in Kampong Glam (see pg 80), they flip and fill the *roti* dough at the front of the restaurant so you can stand and salivate before you get down to serious business. The skilled cooks add more egg than other places and sprinkle the top of their meaty *murtabak* with extra minced meat – these things are epic. But not pretty – it's the sort of food locally called *ho jia bo ho kua* or "tasty but not attractive". Come hungry.

23

Coffee o'clock

At times, Singapore can feel like a shiny, Westernised retail playland where it's a trick to remember you're actually in South-East Asia. When you crave a dose of earthy grit and a whiff of authenticity, head to a *kopi tiam*, or coffee shop.

A TYPICAL, OLD-SCHOOL
KOPI TIAM INTERIOR

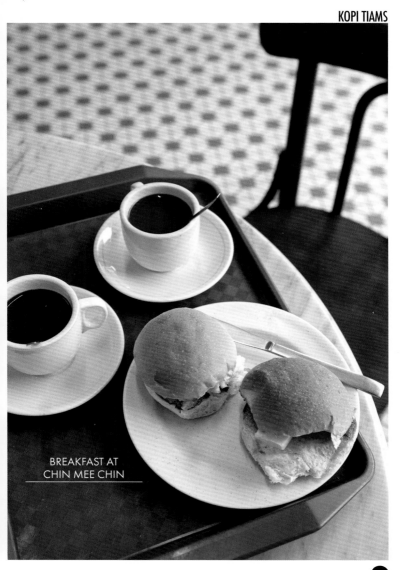

BREAKFAST AT
CHIN MEE CHIN

KOPI TIAMS

These are where locals, particularly older ones, hang out over tea, coffee and simple, cheap food, reading newspapers, chatting or just catching a breather. Especially around breakfast time. Apart from *roti prata* (see pg 18), the quintessential Singapore breakfast consists of toasted white, fluffy bread (or buns), spread with lashings of *kaya* (coconut and egg jam flavoured with pandan), fortified with slabs of cold butter. Alongside, you inevitably get two half-cooked eggs; these you liquidise with a spoon, adding ground pepper and soy sauce to taste. You dip your toast into the runny, seasoned eggs as you eat it. Those eggs, which are gloopy (unset whites! shudder!), can be a hard sell to the uninitiated, although the toast and *kaya* combo is universally pronounced sensational. Such English-derived foods came from cooks who'd formerly worked in colonial households but left their positions to set up their own *kopi tiams*.

At the heart of the Singapore *kopi tiam* is the coffee *(kopi)* itself, made using freshly roasted Robusta beans, which are better suited to growing in South-East Asia. High in caffeine, these are not as subtle tasting as Arabica beans, which are considered higher quality, with more complex flavours. But here's the thing – in Singapore, the beans are roasted with dashes of margarine or butter, and sometimes sugar, which lend caramelised tones to the finished product. The Hainanese, who perfected this style of roasting, developed it to make the Robusta beans taste better – without the butter-added sweetness, they'd be ▷

THE KOPI TIAM LOWDOWN

Kopi: the default. Black coffee sweetened with condensed milk. The taste for tinned milk comes from earlier times when the fresh equivalent was a rarity – even though it's readily available these days, locals still prefer the sweet, sticky (or evaporated) canned stuff in their *kopi* and tea.

Kopi-o: with sugar but no milk

Kopi-o kosong: no milk or sugar

Kopi kosong: evaporated milk but no sugar (*kosong* means 'plain')

Kopi-c: (also *kopi si*) made with unsweetened evaporated milk and sugar, and less sweet than straight *kopi*. 'C' is for 'Carnation', the iconic brand of canned evaporated milk.

Kopi-c kosong: with evaporated milk but no sugar

Kopi peng: iced coffee with milk and sugar

Coffee: DON'T ask for this. You'll get a mug of instant Nescafe. Truly!

You can request your coffee strong (*gao*) or weak (*poh*), either with or without milk. Or 'more sweet' (*ga dai*) or 'less sweet' (*siew dai*). The exact same terms apply to tea (*teh*). With two specific exceptions – *teh halia* is sweet, spicy ginger tea, made using fresh ginger, tea and lashings of condensed milk. And milky *teh tarik*, which is the traditional Malay 'pulled' tea. It's foamy and rich, and made by pouring the hot tea (comprising strong black tea with either condensed or evaporated milk) between two vessels from a height, to create the characteristic creamy texture and foamy surface.

KNOW YOUR KOPI

coffee
sugar

KOPI-O

coffee
with no
milk or
sugar

KOPI-O KOSONG

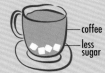
coffee
less
sugar

KOPI-O SIEW DAI

coffee
more
sugar

KOPI-O GA DAI

coffee
sugar
evaporated
milk

KOPI-C

coffee
less sugar
evaporated
milk

KOPI-C SIEW DAI

coffee
more sugar
evaporated
milk

KOPI C GA DAI

coffee
condensed
milk

KOPI

strong
coffee
condensed
milk

KOPI GAO

coffee
ice
condensed
milk

KOPI PENG

very
strong coffee
condensed
milk

KOPI DI LO

weak
coffee
condensed
milk

KOPI POH

KOPI TIAMS

acrid and bitter. As it is, *kopi* tastes decidedly chocolately and rich, and benefits from the addition of sweetened condensed, or evaporated milk.

A *kopi tiam* might have its own, secret roasting technique or recipe. Throw in the brewing method (grounds are brewed in tall metal pots inside a fabric 'sock', through which water filters to produce a strong, dense drink), and you get a coffee with plenty of taste, character and kick. Locals are particular about where they go for their *kopi* and even who makes it; just as you might have your favoured barista at home. BTW, you'll easily find espresso around town, in case you feel the need for Western-style coffee.

Pouring freshly brewed *kopi*

There's some interesting lore around *kopi tiams*. For example, when gambling was outlawed in Singapore in 1829, the coffee houses became fronts for illegal betting dens. They attracted gangs – some owners had false walls installed so gangs could meet in secret. ◆

> Ordering *kopi* like a Singapore boss requires a whole new language.

Classic *kopi* cups

WHERE TO KOPI

TONG AH EATING HOUSE
35 Keong Saik Road.
6.30am-10pm (closed alt Weds)
You'd never know this place is more than 70 years old, as a recent relocation has been at the expense of the original scruffy charm, but hey. Now there's aircon. The white toast is legendary – order it steamed or triple toasted, for ultra crispness. And their *kaya* – deep green from fresh pandan – is held to be one of the best versions in Singapore. Owner Tang Chew Fue is the forth generation in his family to run the place.

KILLINEY KOPITIAM
67 Killiney Road.
6am-11pm Mon, Wed, Sat, 6am-6pm Tues and Sun
It's a franchise now, complete with merch and multiple outlets, but the history goes back to 1919. As such, it's the oldest existing Hainanese coffee shop in town (the name isn't the original, though). *Kopi*, soft toast and *kaya* are all fabulous; go to the original shop on Killiney Road for the best experience. The breakfast menu is more extensive than is the norm; chicken curry with baguette, *laska* and *mee siam* are on offer, for example.

TOAST BOX
#01-45/46 Chinatown Point, 133 New Bridge Road.
8am-10pm, daily
Giving any address for Toast Box is token as there are more than 70 outlets city-wide. But don't be put off by the McDonald's-ish model or slick modernity. With so many locales, you're never far from a dependably great place to queue with locals for *kopi* and *kaya* toast; Toast Box is beloved. Note that their *nasi lemak* (see pg 34) is pretty darnned good too.

CHIN MEE CHIN CONFECTIONERY
204 East Coast Road.
8am-4.30pm Tues-Sun
Service can be a bit gruff at this famously nostalgic place; it occupies a pre-war shophouse and the marble-topped tables and slender wooden chairs are heavily reminiscent of original *kopi tiams*. But once you sink your choppers into their pillowy buns, as it were, slathered with not-too-sweet home-made *kaya* and stuffed with slabs of butter, all will be forgiven. They still heat their coffee over a charcoal stove and bake their own buns – and custard puffs and sausage rolls – daily.

HEAP SENG LEONG
10 North Bridge Road.
4am-7pm, daily
Fans have been whirring, the *kopi*'s been brewing and the Uncles have been slurping their drinks from saucers here for decades. If you really want a vanishing glimpse of what *kopi tiams* used to be like, here's your place. They're famous for *kopi gu you* (coffee with butter), which has a toffee-like taste and is a real rarity these days. Why butter coffee? Because butter used to be expensive in Singapore and having a bit of it in your drink symbolised wealth.

YY KAFEI DIAN
37 Beach Road.
7.30am-9.30pm Mon-Fri, 8am-9.30pm Sat-Sun
A short walk from the Bugis MRT, this old timer is famous for the way they do their *kaya* toast – it's served in a split, home-baked bun that's fluffy inside. The *kaya* is particularly coconutty; and there are other old-fashioned baked goods on offer as well. Plus, they run a menu of Hainan-style dishes, including their signature claypot *ee fu* (egg) noodles and decent chicken rice.

HUA BEE RESTAURANT
#01-19, 78 Moh Guan Terrace, Tiong Bahru.
7am-3pm (closed Mon)
Another old-school treasure in a rustic, weathered space, they've been around for 70-odd years. They are most famous for fish ball *mee pok* (noodles) and *kopi* and toast in the morning. What's also notable about this place is that it's now home to a modern *yakitori* restaurant called Bincho. This is in a discreet little space reached through curtains at the back of the old cafe; you have to be in the know to realise it's even there. They encourage patrons to finish a meal with a *kopi* or *teh* from out front. Cute.

LAKSA AT SLICK,
MODERN QIJI ON
JALAN PESAR

So much a part of the Singaporean woodwork, it's hard to remember that *laksa* is a hybrid dish from the Nyonya school of culinary thinking. What's not hard is to know that no SGP trip is complete without a few rounds of its spicy, slurpy, noodley yumness.

LAKSA

It's also called curry *laksa* or *laksa lemak*, to differentiate it from other types found around this part of the world (such as Sarawak *laksa* and *assam laksa*). 'Lemak' means 'rich' and, in the context of *laksa*, denotes creaminess. The degree of *lemak* depends on the amount of coconut milk used, which can vary. Good *laksa* should have an oomphy, creamy, curried gravy, thick round rice noodles that still have a little bite (overcooked ones are mushy) and a generous dose of cockles, prawns, sliced beancurd puff and maybe some strips of squid. Some places add slices of fish cake, hard-boiled egg or even crab stick bits. On top go some beansprouts and a little finely shredded *laksa* leaf (also known as Vietnamese mint); on your spoon you'll get a blob of chilli-hot *sambal*. You stir this into the gravy before eating – chilli wimps can ask ▷

LAKSA

Laksa with prawn and sliced fish cake

328 Katong Laksa

Serving *laksa*

Depot Road claypot *laksa*

the vendor to hold off if they prefer. The secret to the alluring flavour is quality coconut milk in the broth and a freshly-made – not commercial – curry paste (called a *rempah*) that forms the base of the dish. In this paste are a dozen or so different components – galangal, candlenuts, chillies, lemongrass, shallots, *belacan*, turmeric, garlic, star anise, coriander seed and oil, typically. Recipes vary among vendors so tastes and textures are not identical from *laksa* to *laksa*.

Where things get really interesting is with Katong *laksa*, a wholly Singaporean invention. First concocted by a couple of brothers in a coffee shop in 1963 on East Coast Road in Katong (hence the name), its defining characteristic is that the noodles are chopped into pieces, making it possible to glug down a bowlful using a spoon, not chopsticks. (Ordinarily you use a spoon for the gravy and chopsticks for everything else.) Other than the chopped noodles, it's the same as *laksa lemak*. There are a number of places that serve Katong *laksa* and if you're keen on eating it from the family who first whipped it up, head to Janggut Laksa in the Queensway Shopping Centre (10am-9pm, daily), though you should know it's a little out of the way. ◆

WHERE TO EAT

SUNGEI ROAD LAKSA
#01-100, Blk 27 Jalan Berseh.
3am-5pm (closed Wed)
Fans queue for the good, cheap *laksa* (three bucks at the time of writing) that's cooked the old-fash way – over charcoal. They're in a traditional-style coffee shop and all they do, food-wise, is *laksa*. It's as good as it gets, really.

328 KATONG LAKSA
51 East Coast Road.
10am-10pm, daily
Gordon Ramsay thinks he put this on the map with his 2013 cooking showdown here but ... not so much. Local foodies have loved the balanced *laksa* gravy and delicious *otah*, to eat on the side, forever. Order *laksa* either large or small, with extra house-made *sambal* if you like.

DEPOT ROAD ZHEN SHAN MEI CLAYPOT LAKSA
#0-75 Alexandra Village, 120 Bukit Merah Lane.
9am-4pm (closed Sun)
So thick your chopsticks will nearly stand up in it, their full-throttle gravy is not for the weak of heart – literally. The

veritable carbonara of *laksas*, it's topped with fish cake, prawns, shredded chicken and cockles and the claypot it is served in keeps it piping hot.

QIJI
193 Jalan Besar.
11am-3am, daily
With their slick, modern styling, natural light (yay) and casual canteen vibe, you might think these places are new (there are 14 outlets) but they've been around for 20 years. You can specify your *laksa* noodles, including wholemeal, and serves are large. The broth is less coconut-milky, a concession to the health conscious.

BABA CHEWS BAR AND EATERY
#01-01 Katong Square, 86 East Coast Road.
6.30am-11pm Sun-Thurs, 6.30am-12am Fri-Sat
Housed in the historic Joo Chiat Police Station, they've tarted up traditional Peranakan dishes (see pg 102) with some clean, contemporary plating. The room is lovely; it's the diner for Hotel Indigo. At nearly $20, the *laksa* is Up There, but it does have scallops and a stunningly balanced prawn-based gravy.

Scrumptious coconutty rice, smatterings of toasty peanuts, crunched up *ikan bilis* (dried anchovies), juicy bits of cucumber, boiled egg and a splodge of lip-smacking sambal. Sigh. *Nasi Lemak*.

NASI LEMAK

Or 'rich rice', as the direct translation from the Malay goes. If there's a more perfect line-up of textures (soft/crisp/unctuous/chewy/gloopy) and flavours (bright/hot/creamy/salty/fresh/rich), we don't know what they are. The rice isn't just infused with coconut but with pandan leaf too, sometimes called the 'vanilla' of South-East Asia. The mellow, sweet, herbal deliciousness of these long, spear-like leaves is unmistakable – there's nothing else nothing quite like it.

It's thought that early Malay communities in Singapore living along the coast with access to coconuts (for milk), anchovies and *ikan selar kuning* (a smallish fish that can be fried so crisp you can eat its bones), invented *nasi lemak*. *Kang kong*, or water convolvulus, was another essential side for the original dish. Traditionally wrapped in a tight, pyramid-shaped parcel in banana leaves, *nasi lemak* made a ▷

NASI LEMAK

transportable breakfast or snack for paddy-field workers; as Singapore developed, roving vendors hawked the dish from baskets.

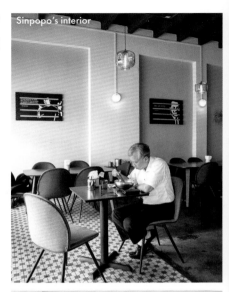
Sinpopo's interior

The rice must be carefully steamed; if cooked directly over high heat, the coconut milk can burn. Many modern cooks use a rice cooker for convenience. Some say you should half cook the rice in water the night before, add the coconut milk and pandan leaves the next morning and then finish cooking, for the best taste. Malay cooks favour Malaysian-grown rice which is starchy, has good chew and is designed for room temperature consumption. Although some like basmati too. Singaporean Chinese cooks lean toward jasmine rice, best eaten warm.

The dish has evolved with increasing wealth and is served with myriad sides; especially the Chinese version. Expect stuff like fried chicken, beef *rendang*, tamarind prawns, packets of *otah* (see pg 50), wedges of omelette, fried eggs, sausage, luncheon meat or fish cakes. Some of these bits are porky, a sacrilegious idea to Malay orthodoxy, which insists on halal food.

THE COCONUT CLUB
椰子俱乐部
KELAB KELAPA
தேங்காய் கிளப்

Essential to a good *nasi lemak* is *sambal tumis belacan*, an umami bomb of chilli, *belacan* (a fermented shrimp paste), shallots, garlic, tamarind, *gula melaka* (palm sugar) and maybe lemongrass and candlenuts, on the side. Malay versions tend to be sweeter and less spicy, to not overpower the rice. ◆

The Coconut Club

Nasi lemak to go

WHERE TO EAT

SELERA RASA NASI LEMAK
#02-2 Adam Road Food Centre, Adam Road.
7am-10pm, daily
You're going to the acclaimed Botanic Gardens, right? (You so should.) This family affair, feted as the best *nasi lemak* in Singapore, is handily close. Those crisp chicken wings and that lovely rice! You order meal sets; go for the Full House for a bit of everything. Among their many accolades is the fact the Sultan of Brunei insists on having food from here every time he's in town.

HI LESKMI NASI LEMAK
#01-24 Whampoa Makan Place, 90 Whampoa Drive.
11am-10pm (closed Sat)
Just off Balestier Road, an interesting street to wander down from a food and architecture perspective, the Whampoa food court has some real gems. Like this one, where you can customise your *nasi lemak* with various sides (including stir-fried eggplant) and where the *sambal,* which has tamarind added, is a customer fav.

NASI LEMAK KUKUS
229 Selegie Road.
12pm-9.30pm (closed Sun)
Close to Little India, here you get to customise and have unlimited rice and *sambal* free. These are self service, so you can pile your plate sky high, and *sambal* comes in two versions, one less heaty. Sides include curries (potato and prawn, egg, beef *rendang*) and a kick-arse chicken wing. They steam rice the old-fashioned way so it's properly infused with coconut.

CHOON'S NASI LEMAK
216-6 Syed Alwi Road.
Open 24 hours, daily
Fairly new, this spick and span place is the brainchild of Mr Ng, from well-known Da Lian Traditional Noodle place at 216G next door. He put his heart and soul into perfecting his *sambal* and the coconut-pandan fragranced rice; choose from simple sets, with chicken wing and *otah* the go-to combo.

THE COCONUT CLUB
6 Ann Siang Hill.
11am-3pm, 6pm-9.30pm Tues-Sat, 11am-3pm Sun
It's good to see a trend towards upmarket, slick versions of street food and Coconut Club does an awesome job of tarting up *nasi lemak* for the corporate masses. Diehards might baulk at spending $10 plus for a plateful but the *ayam goreng* (fried chicken encrusted with *galangal,* turmeric and lemongrass) is worth the price alone. Rice is taken uber seriously – they use old-crop Thai jasmine rice and only buy coconuts from a specific Malay plantation in Selangor, extracting their own coconut milk, in-house. Very impressive.

PONGGOL NASI LEMAK
965 Upper Serangoon Road.
5.30pm-3.30am (closed Thurs)
Long queues at peak times speak to the popularity of this famous eatery. Punters love the large side dish selection, which includes chicken wings, veg curry, fried *sotong* (cuttlefish) fish balls, eggplant and *otah.* The homemade sambal is next level, and regulars rave over the fried crisp skin chicken with curry leaves.

BALI NASI LEMAK
#2 Geylang Lorong 15.
5.30pm-4am (closed alt Sun)
They're famed for their *kecap manis* (sweet soy) chicken wings, the variety of curries, *sambal petai* (spicy stink beans) and the fact that you can get a *nasi lemak* in the wee hours. And for their particularly coconutty rice and the wallet-friendly prices.

SINPOPO
458 Joo Chiat Road.
12pm-10pm Tues-Thurs and Sun, 12pm-12am Fri-Sat
Inspired by local nostalgia but unabashedly hipster-grade groovy, Sinpopo is adorable. They're known for cakes but run a small menu that includes a now-famous NL. It's for two and comes with marinated pork belly, fried wings, *rojak* slaw, luncheon meat crisps, soft-centered eggs and *sambal* fish balls. Phew.

Hawker Centres

Singapore is slick, sophisticated and ... constantly hungry. The restless masses seem permanently on the prowl for their next fix of XXX (insert the name of any number of contenders, covering noodles, soups, roast meats, snacks, salads, breads, drinks and sweets). Instead of greeting each other with a 'hi', locals say *'sudah makan?'*, or 'have you eaten?'. That's how food obsessed they are. And, despite the city's gleaming polish and stupefying number of extremely smart/ very smart/smart-casual dining choices, the natives have never lost their love for the humble hawker. It's to a hawker centre they invariably rush when the urge to eat strikes, yet again.

RICE PORRIDGE (CONGEE), UBIQUITOUS FOR BREAKFAST

MAXWELL FOOD
CENTRE

HAWKER CENTRES

Singapore may be affluent now but in the post-war 1950s and 1960s, folk here struggled and unemployment was rife. Many took their pots, woks and blocks of *belacan*, hit the streets and freelance cooked for dosh; this was an accessible self-employment option as hawking didn't require much to set up, and good income could be had. Most itinerant cooks specialised in one, or a couple of dishes only. By the late 1960s, the number of food hawkers had ballooned to 24,000 and what resulted was a literal movable feast ... plus a host of dire sanitation issues. With no direct water supply on the street, utensils, plates and cooking gear couldn't be kept clean and food waste was dumped straight into open drains. Yuck.

In stepped the government, relocating vendors to purpose-built centres with proper amenities, making them centralised, sanitary and regulated. Centres were built into burgeoning public housing estates, called 'heartlands', providing dining facilities for the swathes of people moving in. These estates, and their hawker centres, are still part of the Singaporean fabric to this day. By the mid-1980s, 140 such hawker centres had been constructed; the last true hawker was hoofed off the streets in 1985.

Today, the National Environment Agency, responsible for hawker oversight, manages around 190 food markets and centres – that's more than 15,000 stalls. The Agency grades individual food sellers annually, bestowing A, B, C or D ratings for cleanliness; certificates are displayed prominently at each stall. Hawker centres vary in size and are generally semi-enclosed and cooled by fans. They have a distinctly unpretentious community buzz and you'll find one near practically every transport hub. And in major housing estates. There, you'll see the entire Singapore demography – from suited corporates, retirees and giggling schoolgirls to labourers and hipster youth – all eating cheek by jowl.

In a centre, each stall specialises in one, or a few related dishes and some hawkers have long cooking pedigrees going back generations. Lines form at outlets that are particularly renowned (although some suggest Singaporeans simply enjoy queueing!) and Michelin has even got in on the act, dishing out its coveted Bib Gourmand awards to standout hawkers. Locals gravitate to their favourite centres and their favoured dishes, the range of which is mind blowing. This is thanks to a mash-up of influences, primarily Malay, Chinese and Indian. Quality, for the (generally) low prices, tends to be high across the board.

More hawker centres are planned, but with the median age of hawker cooks now hovering around the early 60s, and younger generations tending to spurn this work for office jobs, questions remain as to how hawking will continue into the future. Will some of the more labour-intensive dishes survive? Take *kway*

HAWKER CENTRES

chap (rice noodles in a dark soy sauce broth with offal, duck, and beancurd), for example, where intestines need to be painstakingly cleaned by hand. Standing over a wok to fry *char kway teow* (rice noodles with soy, prawns, cockles, egg and sprouts) is ridiculously hard and back-breaking work; who wants to do that long term? Some dishes, such as *muah chee* (nuggets of glutinous rice flour dough tossed in sugar and crushed peanuts) have almost disappeared altogether – the dish might sound artless, but stirring the super-thick dough over low heat for 1½ hours until it achieves just the right consistency is a punish. But, leave it to the clever Singaporeans – they'll work something out to ensure the future of thriving centres. Singapore without hawkers just wouldn't be right. ◆

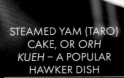

STEAMED YAM (TARO)
CAKE, OR *ORH
KUEH* – A POPULAR
HAWKER DISH

HAWKER CENTRES

1. Char kway teow

2. Mung bean pudding

3. Fish hor fun

4. Appam

5. Sambal stingray

6. Popiah

7. Black carrot cake

8. Bak chang

HAWKER CENTRES

9. Curry chicken bee hoon

10. Braised duck noodles

11. Prawn fritters

12. Fish ball noodles

13. Steamed cassava cake

14. Otah otah

15. Cuttlefish kang kong

16. Kway chap

HAWKER CENTRES

17. Rojak

18. Fried bee hoon

19. Yong tau foo

20. Tofu pudding

21. Mee siam

22. Lor mee

23. Chwee kueh

24. Indian rojak

HAWKER CENTRES

25. Braised pork hock

26. Roast pork

27. Curry puffs

28. Mango sago pudding

29. Bak chor mee

30. Durian ice kacang

31. Bao

32. Cendol

What to Hawker

The names here are the most commonly used ones, hence the mix of English, Malay and Chinese. This list is by no means exhaustive, but it covers many of the dishes and snacks you'll encounter when you're out and about.

1. Char kway teow: fresh, broad rice noodles stir fried with egg, prawns, cockles, sprouts and, sometimes, Chinese sausage. A good CKT balances sweet, salty, crunchy and chewy with *wok hei* (smoky-wokky flavour).

2. Mung bean pudding: called *tau sau* in Chinese. It's sweetened with sugar, spiked with pandan and thickened with water chestnut flour. Served warm or hot and topped with slices of *youtiao* (fried dough sticks).

3. Fish hor fun: *hor fun* is the Cantonese name for fresh, broad rice noodles. The noodles are stir fried then served with the thick, gravied fish mixture spooned over the top. There are lots of variants, notably beef.

4. Appam: cooked in a special curved pan to give the characteristically thick middle and thin, lacy edges, the batter for this pancake is made from fermented rice and coconut. Served with sugar and coconut milk.

5. Sambal stingray: also called *ikan bakar* (Malay for 'grilled fish'). Stingray has a particularly meaty texture and in this classic dish it's grilled in a thick, gutsy spice paste then served on banana leaf. #beerfood

6. Popiah: a fresh spring roll made using a very thin, wheat-flour wrapper. Filled with seasoned tofu, shredded vegetables like yam bean and carrot, and egg, lettuce and prawn.

7. Black carrot cake: cubes of radish cake fried in a wok with beaten egg, garlic and green onion and maybe prawn. There are two versions: 'white' carrot cake is fried atop beaten egg which forms a wonderful crust; while the 'black' one mixes the egg in and adds sweet soy sauce.

8. Bak chang: a type of big dumpling made by stuffing glutinous rice with various fillings (pork, salted egg, sweet bean paste etc). Wrapped in bamboo leaves, it's steamed.

9. Curry chicken bee hoon: a coconut milk-based soup noodle dish, chunky with tender, poached chicken, potatoes and slices of tofu puff, with a rich *sambal* to add. Ah Heng (531A, Upper Cross Street, #02-58, Hong Lim Food Centre) do a cracker version.

10. Braised duck noodles: Teochew-styled braised duck in a dark, unthickened soy-based sauce, served over egg noodles. The duck is served boned – the bones are used to make the stock served as soup on the side or poured over the noodles.

11. Prawn fritters: flour-based crisp snacks; some contain corn or green onion as well as prawn. They're usually served in pieces, dipped into chilli sauce.

12. Fish ball noodles: good fish balls (and fish cakes) are homemade, light and springy, served with various noodles *(bee hoon*/rice vermicelli or *mee pok*/flat egg noodles), in soup or with soup on the side. Find a critically acclaimed fish ball or two at Fishball Story, 01-14, 73A Ayer Rajah Crescent.

13. Steamed cassava cake: made by steaming a mixture of grated fresh cassava (tapioca root), fresh coconut, sugar, tapioca flour and coconut milk then cutting the soft, chewy cake into small pieces and rolling in grated coconut. Sometimes colour is added.

14. Otah otah: a thin fish cake made by mixing ground fish (and sometimes squid and prawn) with spice paste and rice flour. Wrapped in banana leaf then grilled, it's eaten alone or served with *nasi lemak* or *laksa*.

15. Cuttlefish kang kong: blanched cuttlefish and water convolvulus (*kang kong*), with vermicelli and various garnishes (sesame, pineapple, carrot). It's slicked with a heavy, thick, sweet sauce and chopped peanuts and is a Singapore invention.

16. Kway chap: offalistas – hold your hats. Here are all The Pig Parts (intestines, skin, belly) in a dark soy-based mixture with egg, tofu and maybe fish cake, served with rice or noodles and plenty of cooking sauce. Like many hawker dishes, the extact composition varies.

17. Rojak: meaning 'mixture', *rojak* is a chunky salad of crisp vegetables (cucumber, yam bean) and slightly unripe fruits (pineapple, guava, mango), smothered in a thick, sweet-spicy dressing based on pungent prawn paste. Can contain *sotong* (squid), tofu puffs and slices of fried dough stick.

18. Fried bee hoon: also called 'economy noodles', these are a favoured breakfast filler-upper. Topped with various *liao* (ingredients) such as fried egg, luncheon meat or cabbage, the noodles can vary. Choose flat rice (*kway teow*), egg or *bee hoon* (vermicelli) or a mixture of two or three. Filling!

19. Yong tau foo: vegetables, mushrooms and tofu chunks, stuffed with fish paste then cooked and served either dry with sauce or in soup. Filling variants include pork mince; the vegetables used are of the eggplant, bitter gourd, okra and capsicum ilk.

20. Tofu pudding: *tau huay* in Hokkien, this pillow-soft and refreshing dish is made by coagulating soy milk. Only lightly sweetened, it's topped with a variety of bits and bobs, from peanuts to candied fruits. A clear, sweet syrup traditionally is drizzled over.

21. Mee siam: one of many, many noodle dishes, this one's inspired by Thai flavours. The gravy is light, spicy, sweet and sour, spiked with tamarind and salted soy paste. Typically topped with shredded omelette or egg, sprouts, tofu and green onion.

22. Lor mee: toothsome yellow wheat noodles with a range of meaty/fishy/eggy items (depending on the stall) drowned in a hefty, starch-thickened gravy with chilli sauce.

23. Chwee kueh: a rice-flour cake steamed in special, shallow cup-like containers. Served with chopped preserved radish and chilli sauce and popular for breakfast. Seek out Jian Bo Shui Kueh at Tiong Bahru Hawker Centre (see pg 53).

24. Indian rojak: also called *pasembur*, Indian *rojak* features bits of fritter (prawn, commonly), boiled egg, potato and cucumber pieces, sprouts, onion etc. Drenched in rich peanut and chilli sauces the precise composition of the dish varies among vendors.

25. Braised pork hock: a typical southern-Chinese influenced hawker dish made by simmering pork hock (or trotters) in spice-infused masterstock. Served with rice, it's as much about the texture of the soft, sexy skin as it is about the sweet nuggets of meat.

26. Roast pork: classic Cantonese roasted pork, with juicy flesh, melty fat and super-crisp skin. You'll also see the full complement of southern Chinese BBQ meats; BBQ pork (*char siu*), roast ducks etc.

27. Curry puffs: with their sturdy, flaky pastry and thick curry filling (chicken and potato, generally) these are thought to have origins in English cooking. Look for outlets of Old Chang Kee, an old brand that's now a franchise, selling their puffs and other snacks.

28. Mango sago pudding: a simple Chinese-style dessert and one of many cooling sweets. It's made using cooked sago pearls, evaporated milk, sugar and chopped mango – there's also a variant made with pomelo.

29. Bak chor mee: 'minced meat noodles' doesn't really cover it; this has the mince, plus pork slices, liver, mushroom, meatballs, wontons and deep-fried lard bits. Choose a dry or soup version; check out Michelin-awarded Hill Street Tai Hwa (#01-12, 466 Crawford Lane), for Singapore's finest.

30. Durian ice kacang: literally 'bean ice'. A tower of finely shaved iced is drenched in rose, or other syrup and evaporated milk. And topped with things like corn, kidney beans, grass jelly, *cendol*, agar agar cubes and maybe ice-cream. Durian, and other seasonal fruits, are also popular additions. *Ice kacang* is wonderfully cooling.

31. Bao: steamed Chinese buns made from leavened dough, stuffed with everything from pork, green vegetables, salted egg, sweet bean and custard. An excellent breakfast.

32. Cendol: said as 'chen-dol', this sweet treat gets its name from the green, worm-like rice flour strips that are characteristic. Along with the shaved ice and the *cendol* (flavoured with pandan) there are kidney beans, rich coconut milk and lashings of gooey *gula melaka* (palm sugar) syrup.

How to Hawker

Lunch and dinner hours are frantic
and it's strictly 'first in first seated'. Reserve a seat by putting a pack of tissues, or a pen, on a table. Reserving thus is to 'chope' in local lingo. Do NOT take a seat already claimed!

Peruse the various stalls then decide on what you fancy
Line up to order and pay – some places will deliver your food to your table but many will display 'self service' signs, signifying that you have to collect the cooked food yourself. You get a tray for this.

Food is fixed price and cash only

You'll share a table when a centre is busy ... and this is part of the fun.

Bring your own hand wipes
Some hawker fare can be messy (and stainy) to eat. There will be a basin and tap outside somewhere for washing too.

Do not encourage the birds!
Pigeons in Singapore are bold to the point of Hitchcockian aggression.

The various stalls in a hawker centre will keep their own opening hours;
they're not consistent throughout a centre.

WHERE TO HAWKER

MAXWELL FOOD CENTRE
1 Kadayanallur Street. Once a wet market, this turned into a temporary home for the China Street food vendors in the 1980s. It's remained a hawker centre since. Close to the CBD, it's popular with city workers, featuring a range of Singaporean-style Chinese dishes. Famous stalls include Zhen Zhen Porridge (for rice porridge), Tian Tian Hainanese Chicken Rice and Jin Hua Fish Head Bee Hoon.

NEWTON CIRCUS FOOD CENTRE
500 Clemenceau Avenue North.
Built in 1971, this recently renovated centre is very pleasant, drawing both local office workers and tourists alike. It's known particularly for barbecue seafood stalls; about 30 of the 80 stalls here grill fish et al. Other notable outlets include Kwee Heng, with more than 50 years of serving its braised and roast meat dishes, and Bee Heng, which has been making *popiah* since the 1920s. For seafood, try Alliance, three decades old and a recent Michelin awardee.

OLD AIRPORT ROAD FOOD CENTRE
Block 51, #0-91 Old Airport Road.
Built around 40 years ago and with 150-odd stalls,

this is one of Singapore's largest centres. It's near the Dakota stop on the MRT so is easily accessible. It has many notable tenants; 50-year-old Chuan Kee Satay, Toa Payoh Rojak and Dong Ji Fried Kway Teow among them. Oh, and Xin Mei Xiang Lor Mee, where long lines form for their iconic *lor mee*.

REDHILL FOOD CENTRE
85 Redhill Lane.
A local institution in one of Singapore's oldest housing estates, built in 1955. Firmly out of the tourist zone (but not far from the CBD – catch the MRT to Redhill), prices are low and portions large. Look for Yan, whose fried chicken wings are acclaimed, Seng Heng Braised Duck and Redhill Curry Rice, the most popular of the three curry rice stalls.

TIONG BAHRU FOOD CENTRE
30 Seng Poh Road.
Rebuilt with art deco lines in 2004 in keeping with the heritage neighbourhood (see pg 92), there are 80 or so stalls here. Many of them were tenants from the original centre. Light-filled and breezy, there's a fantastic selection on offer; beeline to Jian Bo Shui Kueh, the oldest *chwee kueh* stall in Singapore. Or Tian Tian Yuan Dessert House, offering more than 80 hot and iced desserts. Stalwart Hui Ji Fishball Noodles & Yong Tau Fu serves ultra-sweet handmade fish balls.

WHAMPOA MAKAN PLACE
91 Whampoa Drive.
There are three, single-storey blocks here; one (Block 92) is a wet market. Mostly, Block 91 has morning foods while Block 90 services the lunch and dinner throngs. Whampoa Satay Bee Hoon in Block 90 is one of the few places in Singapore serving noodles with satay sauce – delicious. Teochew Kway Teow Mee (Block 91) produces flavoursome bowls of rice noodle soup, while Tanglin Halt A1 Carrot Cake (also Block 91) cooks both black and white versions of the dish, excellently.

TEKKA CENTRE
665 Buffalo Road.
It's in Little India (see pg 79) so no surprises that Muslim and subcontinental dishes feature more than is normal. (There are still plenty of Chinese offerings here though). It's nicely chaotic at busy times and those in the know go for the *biryani* (from Allauddin's Biryani) and tiffin dishes (Anna Dosai and Pandi Ayya Tiffin Centre).

CHOMP CHOMP FOOD CENTRE
20 Kensington Park Road.
This centre is nighttime only, opening at 6pm. Expect evening favourites like satay (Chomp Chomp Satay) and BBQ stingray (Boon Tat Street BBQ Seafood). Tucked into an

area of low-rise homes, the wonderful al fresco setting is perfect on a hot, sticky evening. Just don't come too late or it'll be overly crowded, and smoky.

HONG LIM MARKET AND FOOD CENTRE
531A Upper Cross Street.
Built in 1978, this not-so-famous centre is a calmer, cleaner bet than the huge one in the nearby Chinatown Complex. It services the surrounding CBD so is best for breakfast and lunch as many vendors close in the evening. Hwee Kee, in operation since 1958, serves jellied pork, a rarity these days. Tuck Kee Sah Hor Fun adds crayfish and lobster to the classic *hor fun* (instead of the more usual beef or fish), and Hiong Kee Dumpling's *bak chang* (glutinous rice dumplings) are touted as being among Singapore's top three.

AMOY STREET FOOD CENTRE
7 Maxwell Road.
One of the few centres in the CBD, it gets crowded in here at lunch, when most of the stalls are open. It's been around since 1983 but among the old-timer stalls are some new generation ones too, serving things like salads, muffins and ramen. Hoo Kee Bak Chang serve some of the tastiest *bak chang* in town; the elderly owner at Guo Ya Yin has been making *kway chap* for decades.

A THORNY TOPIC

"Oh yeah, I kinda like durian." Said no one ever. You either love it, or you abso-freaking loathe it. Infamously stinky, the so-called 'King of Fruits' is wildly popular in Singapore, where specimens are mainly imported from neighbouring Malaysia. Even the landmark Esplanade building is nicknamed The Durian, for its distinctively thorny exterior and rounded, durian-like shape.

猫山王
100% Good 包
云顶高原来
1粒 $28b

CHIN YONG FRUITS TRADING CHIN YONG FR

猫生

Large, with a browny-greenish spike-covered husk, inside are fat lobes of yellow/orange flesh. Yes, durian give off a distinctive smell (caused by various ketones, esters and sulphur compounds), but they also have a seductive, custardy texture and the most intriguing flavour.

From a species known as Durio, there are various genus and cultivars of durian; popular types in Singapore include Mao Shan Wang (also called 'Cat Mountain King'), Jin Feng (or 'Golden Phoenix'), the D24 (or 'Sultan'), 'Red Prawn' (also called Ang Hay) and the 'Black Pearl' (or Hei Zhen Zhu). Trees are huge, some reaching heights of 50 metres; the fruits are harvested only when they fall from the trees. Durian are a heavy fruit, with an average weight of 1.5kg, and nets are used to catch them in commercial orchards. Walking under a non-netted tree can be dangerous – you don't want one of these things dropping on your head, although locals do forage for the fruits off wild trees growing around Singapore.

The season for durian is around June to August (although you can get them year round), which coincides with the mangosteen season. Chinese medicinal wisdom has it that you eat mangosteen (said to be 'cooling') to counteract the 'heating' effects of durian. Nutritionally speaking, durian flesh is comprised of 27% carbs, 5% fat and 1% protein – it's rich in thiamin and also contains B and C vitamins and the minerals manganese, potassium, zinc and even calcium.

If you plan to partake (good on you!) you need to go to a reputable seller. Fruits are not cheap and shifty practices exist, such as spraying sub-par or underripe fruits with durian-flavoured water to enhance the aroma. You can either buy a whole fruit and have the vendor crack it open for you, or buy a tray of flesh, ready to go. ◆

WHERE TO EAT DURIAN

COMBAT DURIAN
249 Balestier Road.
12pm-10pm, daily

227 KATONG DURIAN
227 East Coast Road, Katong.
10.30am-10.30pm, daily

SINDY DURIAN
#01-835, Block 89
Whampoa Drive.
Open 24 hours

AH SENG DURIAN
#01-119 – #01-122 Ghim Moh Market,
20 Ghim Moh Road.
12.30pm-10.30pm
Mon-Fri, 12.30pm-7pm
Sat-Sun

WAN LI XIANG
Block 7, 13 Dempsey Road.
3pm-12am, daily

MAO SHAN WANG CAFE
49 Temple Street.
11am-10.30pm
Mon-Wed, 11am-11pm
Thurs-Sat
A cafe dedicated to all things durian. Seriously. The menu features everything from French fries and chicken nuggets with durian sauce, durian coffee, durian Napoleon, durian cream puffs to durian charcoal-crust pizza. Yep, durian pizza. #onlyinSingapore

MULTI-COLOURED
XIAO LONG BAO,
CANTON PARADISE

Dim sum, yum cha, morsels of ridiculous deliciousness … whatever you call this snacking, grazing meal that's Guangzhou's greatest gift to the world, you can indulge in Singapore, big time. From character-filled, good-value stalwarts to elegant, swellegant hotel diners, *yum cha* is easy to find.

DIM SUM

Yum cha is from the literal Cantonese words for 'drink tea' and the practice of eating tasty tidbits with tea hails from southern China, dating from the mid-19th century. It's a leisurely meal, intended for morning or early afternoon consumption, during which you eat *dim sum* (snacks) with your tea. These come in a notably huge range of steamed, simmered, fried and baked iterations, both sweet and savoury. Popular items include *ha gaau* (steamed prawn dumplings in a translucent rice-flour skin); *siu maai* (pork mince and prawns in an open-topped, steamed dumpling); a lacy deep-fried taro dumpling filled with mushrooms called *wuh gok*; slippery pork and prawn steamed rice noodle rolls (*cheong fun*); BBQ pork buns (*cha siew bao*) either steamed or baked; steamed sticky rice in lotus leaf (*noh mai gai*); sweet egg tarts (*daahn taat*); tofu pudding (*dauh fuh fa*); mango pudding (*monggwo* ▷

DIM SUM

Cute steamed custard buns

A selection of steamed *dim sum*

家酒星紅
請由此進
RED STAR

A chef at Red Star

YUM CHA

Yum Cha Restaurant

AT THE FULLERTON
HOTEL'S GORGEOUS
JADE RESTAURANT

DIM SUM

boudin); and tofu skin rolls (*fu pei guen*). And on and on and on and so on. There are many, many types.

The traditional service of *dim sum*, still seen in a handful of old-time places, is rather unique. In the 1960s, push carts with heated, steamy compartments for keeping food hot became the popular way to ferry food to customers – before this, servers roamed a dining room carrying food in baskets. You pick out only what you want from the passing parade, in the spirit of a moving smorgasbord. These days you are more likely to order by ticking items off a printed card – this system reduces food waste and means food is cooked fresh and served hotter. It also means that more tables can be squished into a restaurant, and you don't get to salivate as trolleys rumble past ... a shame, really. Items will be listed in English as well as Chinese so ordering isn't hard. Deciding exactly what and how much to have is the tricky part but it's a good idea to order some steamed, some fried and some baked items, for the full textural experience. You'll be offered different teas to drink with your meal, including jasmine, *oolong*, chrysanthemum, *pu'er* (a dark fermented tea called *bo lei* in Cantonese) and even maybe lychee. Chinese tend to favour *pu'er* as a *yum cha* drink, as it's said to 'cut the grease'. Good to know.

Yum cha in Singapore developed thanks to influxes of southern Chinese immigrants and has become a beloved mainstay of the food scene. Singaporean *yum cha* adds Shanghainese snacks like *xiao long bao* (soup dumplings) and drunken chicken plus Sichuan dishes such as chilli oil wontons and spring onion pancakes to the mix. There are local inventions too. Some places, especially hotels, get inventive with their snacks, creating non-standard offerings using ingredients like foie gras, truffles, mayonnaise, squid ink and mango. Ask a Singaporean what their favourite *dim sum* are and chances are *liu sha bao* will be on the list. This decadent steamed bun with a hot, oozing centre of molten custard and salted duck egg yolk is a wholly local twist. ◆

60

WHERE TO EAT

The complete opening hours are given here but in most instances, *dim sum* will only be served during the morning and early afternoon dining slots.

JADE
The Fullerton Hotel, 1 Fullerton Square.
11am-2.30pm, 6.30pm-10.30pm Mon-Fri, 12pm-2.30pm, 6.30pm-10.30pm Sat-Sun
When you want to kick back in one of the city's most gorgeous (and calming) dining rooms, and feast on text-book perfect fare, here's your place. Surprisingly affordable, given the level of luxe, the *yum cha* menu boasts more than 50 items, including finessed esoterica like foie gras and truffle *ha gaau*, sea urchin *siu maai* and adorable lotus paste pastry flowers. Completely unmissable. On the weekend they feature a Gourmet Dim Sum Treasure menu; the desserts, decorated with hand-crafted embellishments made using gelatine, are something to behold.

YUM CHA RESTAURANT
#02-01, 20 Trengganu Street.
10.30am-10.30pm Mon-Fri, 9am-10.30pm Sat-Sun
Functional, a bit boisterous when busy, but nicely laidback, this place is on a floor above the Chinatown

craziness. Come for the good value *dim sum* buffet (3pm-6pm daily) or the big range (around 60) of à la carte items – like the pumpkin yam cake, mango prawn sesame fritters and squid ink dumplings.

SWEE CHOON TIM SUM
191 Jalan Besar.
11am-2.30pm, 6pm-6am Mon-Sat, 10am-3pm, 6pm-6am Sun
Another nostalgic option near Little India, they've been wrapping dumplings and steaming chickens' feet for 50-odd years. The extended hours make this a perfect destination for night owls. It's not posh. Think blinding downlights, Formica tables and food brought to tables on battered metal trays. Their signature dish is *mee suah kueh* – carrot cake encrusted with a tangle of fine noodes, then fried.

MOUTH
#01-61 China Square Central, 22 Cross Street.
11.30am-3pm, 6pm-10pm Mon-Fri, 10am-3.30pm, 6pm-10pm Sat-Sun
The *liu sha bao* here is baked, not steamed, giving it a crunchy top that's quite unique. A beloved local, the offerings are varied and freshly made daily. Check out rainbow-hued *ha gaau* (prawn dumplings); a basket of seven arrives, each with a different coloured skin, tinted using natural ingredients, such as sweet

potato (orange), squid ink (black) and spinach (green).

RED STAR RESTAURANT,
#07-23, 54 Chin Swee Road.
7am-3pm, daily
This place is true blue old school, there's no denying. Up a creaky elevator in a bland apartment block, the chef here has connections to Chef Lup Chen, considered one of the best Cantonese chefs in 1950s Singapore. His disciples are credited with inventing dishes like *yu sheng*, a raw fish-based celebration dish popular for Chinese New Year. Cart-pushing ladies still ply the room and recipes and presentation are said to be unchanged for 40-odd years; the egg tarts are baked fresh and punters love 'em here. It's the earliest opening of the lot, making *dim sum* for breakfast a distinct reality.

TUNGLOK TEAHOUSE
#01-01 Far East Square, 7-13 Amoy Street.
11.30am-3pm, 6pm-10.30pm Mon-Sat, 10am-2.30pm, 6pm-10.30pm Sun
Dim sum are available for lunch and dinner at this nostalgic diner – 1950s Chinese movie posters grace the walls and there are other period details sprinkled around too. The *dim sum* are all old-school types – *siu maai*, chickens' feet, ribs in black bean, BBQ pork buns and beancurd skin roll with prawns, made fresh

and with great care, daily. There's another outlet at 10 Sinaran Drive – they do set price *dim sum* lunches.

CANTON PARADISE
#01-02 The Shoppes at Marina Bay Sands, 2 Bayfront Avenue.
10.30am-10.30pm Mon-Thurs, 10.30am-11pm Fri-Sun
You're so going to want to shop this gobsmacking mall. Yeah! When you come up for air, eat *dim sum* here. Award winning, they lay claim to inventing multi-coloured *xiao long bao* which are so striking. Flavours include truffle (black), cheese (yellow), ginseng (green) and Sichuan (orangey-pink). The restaurant is part of a family – another is Paradise Dynasty at #04-12A, ION Orchard (2 Orchard Turn).

MAJESTIC BAY RESTAURANT
#01-10, 18 Marina Gardens Drive.
1.30am-3pm, 5.45pm-9pm, daily
Fresh seafood's the specialty, reflected in their signature *dim sum* – a chilli crab meat bun. So good. Set in the Gardens By The Bay complex, the dining room is gloriously light-drenched and modern and the fare is universally fabulous. Order à la carte, or go for the set menu (around $30 a person). Be sure to finish with their other signature, the fun, bright yellow Nutella-filled bun, shaped like a cute little duck.

'Meat bone tea' is the direct translation here, although there's no actual tea in delicious *bak kut teh*. This dish is Singaporean soul food, pure and simple and, if it's not love for you at first slurp, don't give up. It really, really grows on you.

BAK KUT TEH

Bak kut teh is unique to Malaysia and Singapore, although you find it in other Teochew (a Southern Chinese dialect group) strongholds too – southern Thailand, for example. The basic concept is thought to be from Fujian province in China (home of the Hokkien dialect group). Essentially, it's a bowl of punchy broth with a few meaty pork ribs; other ingredients can include offal, egg, mushrooms, greens and garlic cloves. Broth and meat are cooked separately; the broth is made by carefully simmering pork bones. There are two common versions in Singapore – the most popular is the Teochew variant, which was developed before WWII. The broth is light in colour and seasoned with plenty of pepper, a little soy and decent amounts of garlic. Often, you get the choice of upgrading to extra-meaty ribs and this is recommended. Look for '*long gu*' on menus; it's a thick, tender cut with extra fat. As you eat, and your ▷

BAK KUT TEH

soup decreases, staff will wander over with a kettleful to replenish levels.

The other version is the more complex, less common Hokkien type, thought to have developed in the Klang area of Malaysia in the early-20th century. Its broth is hefty and dark, redolent of soy sauce, medicinal herbs and fragrant spices like star anise, cloves, fennel seeds and cassia. It's saltier than the Teochew version and slightly sweet from the addition of rock sugar. Some claim it was the brainchild of a physician and that it was popular with Malaysian port workers, who treated it like a health tonic. Malays and Singaporeans can get prickly over the origins of *bak kut teh* – in 2009, for example, the Malaysian tourism minister claimed that it had been hijacked by neighbouring countries and that it is a wholly Malaysian concept. Halal versions have sprung up in Singapore to cater to Muslim tastes; the meat used in these scenarios varies from mutton and beef through to seafood and ostrich. The usual accompaniments to almost every type of *bak kut teh* are rice and/or sliced *youtiao* (Chinese dough sticks), plus dishes of sliced chilli, soy sauce, minced garlic and chilli sauce for dipping. There's also a dry version of *bak kut teh*, where the broth is boiled down to a thick, gravy consistency; it's a rich, deeply flavoured dish that resembles a braise.

Although technically breakfast food, the lines have blurred and any time of the day or night seems right for *bak kut teh*. You'll find it at hawker centres as well as a number of restaurants that specialise in it; some of these have long pedigrees. ◆

Ng Ah Sio

At Morning Bak Kut Teh

DRY *BAK KUT TEH*
AT LEONG KEE
IN GEYLANG

TEA AND BAK KUT TEH

Oolong tea, served *gong fu* style (which is heart-stoppingly strong) in tiny cups is what you drink with *bak kut teh*. A server makes it in front of you (unless you're confident to DIY), in a wonderfully ritualised fashion. Care is observed in the rinsing of leaves, pot and cups, the right water temperature and the correct brew time. Many *bak kut teh* specialists use tea from purveyors Pek Sin Choon, based in an old shophouse in Chinatown since 1925. You can visit their charming shop (also a retail outlet) where they still hand-wrap individual serves of tea in their characteristic double slips of paper; one white, the other pink. Some of their blends are unchanged since before WWII, and some of these Aunties have been hand-wrapping tea for more than 50 years! BTW, the tea supposedly breaks down the fat in the pork, freshens the palate and elevates the flavour of the soup. **Pek Sin Choon, 36 Mosque Street, Chinatown, 8.30am-6.30pm (closed Sundays)**

Hand-wrapping tea at Pek Sin Choon

66

WHERE TO EAT

SONG FA BAK KUT TEH
11 New Bridge Road.
7am-10pm (closed Mon)
There are seven outlets of this iconic business – their site (www.songfa.com.sg) has details. They started as a hawker cart in 1969 and the shops are infused with tinges of nostalgia that hark back to this time. Their soup and fall-apart-tender ribs are wonderful. They use pepper from Sarawak and a particular type of garlic from China to achieve the glorious flavour.

MORNING BAK KUT TEH
531A Upper Cross Street,
#01-72, Hong Lim Food
Centre.
6am-8pm, daily
In a food centre in Chinatown, behind Chinatown Point and run by an Uncle and a couple of Aunties, they cook the dark, herbal Hokkien version. Ask for soup refills – they're free, as they generally are at all BKT places. The surrounds are a bit earthy, but don't let that deter you. This is great fare, best mopped up with plenty of rice and bits of youtiao (fried dough sticks), and sides like braised peanuts and braised mustard greens.

LEONG KEE BAK KUT TEH
251 Geylang Road.
11am-1am, daily
In vibrant Geylang, with its many great food options,

Leong Kee cook a Hokkien-style *bak kut teh* that some claim is Singapore's best. They serve it in a claypot, so it arrives piping hot, and with vegetables and beancurd skin in the soup alongside pork. The broth is thick and cloudy – they also do a dry version. You can order a mutton or a chicken version if pork doesn't do it for you.

AH TOU BAK KUT TEH
291 Lorong 15, Geylang.
11am-2am, daily
A player from Malaysia, these guys are notable for their divergent BKT styles although, true to their roots, they do a mighty fine Klang (Hokkien)-style BKT. But they also offer a seafood option, which involves clams, prawns, squid, fish, abalone and pork ribs, cooked in a light herbal broth.

RONG CHENG BAK KUT TEH
Blk 26 Sin Ming Lane,
#01-114 Midview City.
9am-9pm, daily
The light broth (no soy sauce) and the DIY tea-brewing, have made this an avowed favourite for nearly 40 years. On weekend mornings, there's a queue so avoid those peak times. They were the first to serve loin ribs, also called 'dragon' ribs, insisting on pork that's hormone and antibiotic free.

NG AH SIO PORK RIBS SOUP EATING HOUSE
208 Rangoon Road.
7am-10pm (closed Mon)
Oh, this place is great. They

opened in 1977 and are known for their particularly peppery, robust broth. Large and barn like, their Xiao Yue Gan tea is recommended as an accompaniment. They're famous for kicking out Thaksin Shinawatra (former Thai Prime Minister) who argued with the owner about his food. Don't do that! They estimate that since opening this branch (1988), they've served more than a million bowls.

LEGENDARY BAK KUT TEH
42 South Bridge Road.
10am-11pm, daily
Legendary achieves true pork perfection; their ribs are really sublime. Now run by the third generation, they source only quality pork and their pepper comes from Sarawak; the Teochew-style stock is delicious. Presentation is a few notches above, too, with a clean modernity that's appealing. There's another branch at 154 Rangoon Road.

FOUNDER BAK KUT TEH
347 Balestier Road.
12pm-2.30am, 6pm-2am (closed Tues)
One of Singapore's iconic outlets. This is the original store but there are franchises too. Founded in 1978 by a local pig farmer, they've honed their version of a Teochew-style broth which has made them famous – pictures of celebrities who dine here grace the walls.

PRAWN NOODLE
SOUP SERVED DRY

A classic hawker dish, these soup noodles are all about the stock. And the noodles. Oh, ok, they're actually all about the prawns too. And the *sambal*. Alright, so they're all about the *sambal*, the noodles and the prawns ... but they're mainly about the stock. Capiche?

PRAWN NOODLE SOUP

To make that lip-smacking, soupy broth, prawn shells and heads are crucial. Everything starts with the browning of pork ribs, bones and even pig's tail in lard, for a little rich colour. Garlic, spices (star anise, cloves, peppercorns) and *ikan bilis* (dried anchovies) are simmered with the pork for two or three hours before prawn shells and heads go in, with a dash of rock sugar. Some cooks like to throw in bit of dried Chinese liquorice, dried orange peel and *lo han* fruit (also called monk fruit), which acts as a natural sweetener. Others add a few secret extras like crab shells or dried scallops. At the end, a little salt or soy sauce is used for seasoning, then the entire batch of strained stock becomes the cooking medium for the prawns. This is an important detail because, as the day wears on and more and more prawns get cooked, that stock concentrates in flavour. Noodles, sprouts, *kang kong* (water ▷

PRAWN NOODLE SOUP

convolvulus) and a dash of *sambal* are the remaining elements. And slices of pork (or the pork ribs from the stock), some fried shallots and, traditionally, small cubes of fried lard. The dish can be served 'dry', with the soup on the side and the noodles tossed in chilli *sambal* in a separate bowl. These days it's fashionable to upscale the dish using jumbo prawns, for which you pay appropriately. Some of these can be massive.

Beach Road Prawn Mee Eating House

It's thought the dish started in the 1880s among immigrants from China's Fujian province. For years the fresh noodles used were made along Hokkien and China Streets in Chinatown, where prawn noodle soup was a popular dish between the 1940s and 1960s. Hokkien noodles, made from wheat flour, are fresh and chewy, resembling thick spaghetti and have a particularly robust texture. This is thanks to alkaline agents that promote chewiness and also give the characteristic yellow colour (this is not from eggs). There will often be *bee hoon* (rice vermicelli) in the mix too. In Singapore you find local and imported prawns on offer and a number of species are preferred for prawn noodle soup. One is the *ang kar* (red leg) with its thin skin and meaty tail and the even more flavoursome *soi kar hei* (green tiger). Wild-caught prawns are a bonus and many prefer their flavour; farmed are more common and cheaper. ◆

Beach Road Prawn Mee Eating House

Jalan Sultan Prawn Mee

WHERE TO EAT

BEACH ROAD PRAWN MEE EATING HOUSE
370 East Coast Road.
8am-4pm (closed Tues)
Famous and popular, this casual eatery occupies two old shophouses. Their stock is not too fishy or salty and there's the option of a wild tiger prawn special, recommended for its deep, umami savour. You can order your soup noodles in small, medium or large sizes and have it 'dry' if you like.

WAH KEE BIG PRAWN NOODLES
#01-15 Pek Kio Food Market and Food Centre 41A Cambridge Road.
7.30am-2pm Wed-Thurs
There's a smart-casual outpost in the CBD now (8 Raffles Avenue, at the base of the Esplanade Mall) but the original has been at the pleasant Pek Kio Food Centre for 65 years. Take your pick. Either way, the secret's in the six types of prawn used to make the meatless stock; this stuff is unadulterated Elixir Of Prawn. Order from regular size all the way to extra large, which will set you back around $30.

JALAN SULTAN PRAWN MEE
2 Jalan Ayer
(off Geylang Lor 1).
8am-3.30pm
(closed Tues)
Succulent jumbo prawns,

PRAWN NOODLE SOUP
tender pork ribs and noodles cooked to *al dente* perfection — this place, though hard to find, is the bee's knees. The soup gets more concentrated as the day wears on so come early if you like it mild and later if you like full-throttle prawniness.

NOO CHENG ADAM ROAD PRAWN MEE
#01-27 Adam Road Food Centre,
2 Adam Road.
9.15am-4pm, 6.30pm-2am, daily
Using huge, wild prawns with sweet, sweet flesh, it's arguable that the dry version here is even better than the soup one. Although. Then again. That stock. It's rich, meaty and prawny, features squid in the mix and gets served with a flourish of crunchy, deep-fried onion.

THE OLD STALL HOKKIEN STREET FAMOUS PRAWN MEE
#02-67 Hong Lim Food Centre, 531A Upper Cross Street.
9am-5pm (closed Thurs)
They don't use MSG and sprinkle the dish with homemade chilli powder, made by frying chilli with dried prawns. They also sell this in jars to take home. The Uncle here reckons they can trace their ancestry back to the original Hokkien Street hawkers; either way it's all delicious.

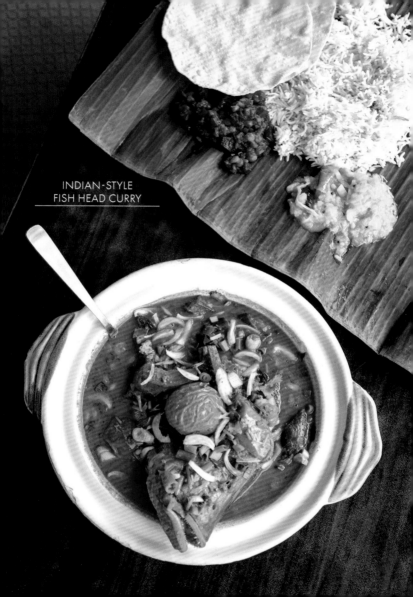

INDIAN-STYLE
FISH HEAD CURRY

Why eat a fish head? Well, fish cheeks, doh. Tender and succulent, the allure of picking at a piscine noggin doesn't stop there, with plenty of other sweet meat to unearth. So please, don't let the appearance of fishy teeth (don't eat), fleshy lips (do eat) and bulging, cooked eyes (eat!) at the table freak you out.

FISH HEAD CURRY

If you spurn fish head curry, you're in bad company – many think this is Singapore's national dish. It was first made in the mid-20th century by a certain M.J. Gomez, an Indian immigrant. He reportedly conjured it to please his Chinese clientele who, he noted, loved eating whole fish, heads included. Gaining wild popularity, the curry was modified by Chinese chefs, who toned down the spicing and pre-steamed the heads, so they don't overcook, before finishing them in a light curry sauce. (In the Indian version, heads are cooked from scratch in a complex curried gravy.) Gomez's original was based on the fish curries of Kerala in India's south. It's common in Indian restaurants to eat the dish, the flesh and sauce scooped from the claypot it's cooked in, off a banana leaf, with mounds of rice, vegetable side dishes and other curries. Whereas in a Chinese situation, it will be shared by diners directly from the claypot. ▷

FISH HEAD CURRY

Chinese-style fish head, in claypot

A large fish head at Zai Shun

At Samy's Curry

White-fleshed species are best for fish head curry, with sea bream and various types of snapper common. Crimson snapper is the ultimate but not as prevalent as goldband or farmed red snapper, which is the cheaper of the three. The gravy can vary, with some cooks adding tamarind for sourness, or coconut milk for smoothness. Heads can be truly massive – up to 1.8kg – and if there are only two or three of you, you'll get a half head, cleavered down the middle before cooking. ◆

WHERE TO EAT

MUTHU'S CURRY
#1-01, 138 Race Course Road.
10.30am-10.30pm, daily
The curry is south Indian in inspiration, with a piquant, deep red sauce. Spiked with okra and pineapple, it isn't overly chilli-hot. The place is run by sons of the founder and every week, when the cooks mix their curry spices, the owners come to oversee the process. The exact recipe is a well-kept secret.

SAMY'S CURRY
25 Dempsey Road.
11am-3pm, 6pm-10pm, daily
Before Dempsey Road was smart, there was Samy's. For more than 50 years it's been enticing folk with flavouricious curry; the fish head one is a knockout. It's eaten off banana leaf harvested from their own garden, with rice (plain or *biryani*), vegetable sides and all the pappadams you can eat.

ZAI SHUN CURRY FISH HEAD
#01-205, 253 Jurong East Street.
7am-3pm (closed Wed)
This humble, but thoroughly excellent eatery is famed for serving the most affordable fresh fish in Singapore and it packs in the punters daily. Their

FISH HEAD CURRY
menu offers so much more than the curry; it's a 'zi char' restaurant, where home-style local Chinese cooking is the thing.

GU MA JIA
45 Tai Thong Crescent.
11am-10pm, daily
The name means 'first Auntie's house' which hints at the vibe – it's very homey and so is the delicious food. They're renowned for *assam* (sour with tamarind) fish head curry. The head comes on a serving plate, not in a claypot, so you don't get so much sauce (dang) but it's beautifully balanced between sweet, sour and savoury (yay).

OCEAN CURRY FISH HEAD
181 Telok Ayer Street.
10.30am-3pm, 5pm-8.30pm (closed Sun)
A bit dearer than is normal, and that's because they use the best quality, large goldband snapper and you simply pay more for that. The Nyonya-style sauce is thick, coconut-rich and full of spicy zip; they cook the head directly in it, so it is infused with all those flavours. If you don't want to pick apart a head, you can have filleted fish pieces in the curry instead. There are many other dishes – *sambal* cockles, black pepper chicken and soy sauce squid to have with rice etc.

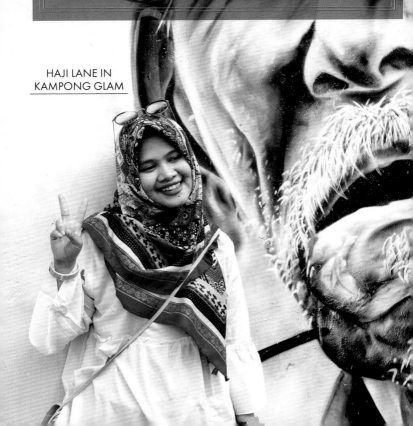

ETHNIC ENCLAVES

If you know nothing else about Singapore, you probably know this – the place is diverse. Malays, Chinese, Indians, South Asians and Europeans all coalesce here in an easy and compelling mishmash. And the city state makes much of its ethnic, religious and cultural harmony.

HAJI LANE IN
KAMPONG GLAM

GOLD JEWELLERY
IN LITTLE INDIA

Sri Veeramakaliamman Temple

Falooda, a cold dessert, in Little India

Ceiling detail, Sri Veeramakaliamman Temple

A temple facade

Suji halwa, a semolina-based sweet

Which isn't to say there aren't distinctly flavoured ethnic enclaves; everyone knows Chinatown, for example. But maybe the two most compelling areas for those wanting to immerse themselves somewhere vaguely exotic for an afternoon or two, are Little India and Kampong Glam.

Of the two, **Little India** is the edgier and grungier. There's an honesty about its heaving streets, busy with **shoppers, tailors, henna artists**, material shops, flower vendors, Hindu worshippers and those on the prowl for a tasty, **subcontinental bite to eat.** It's not as studiously manicured as other parts of the city – not that it's a mess. Keep up, this is Singapore! It's just not as polished, and that can be a relief. It's a **wonderful place to poke around** with no clear agenda.

Singapore's Indians are mostly Tamils, from the south of the mother country, and Little India's origins **go back to the early 1800s.** The first inhabitants were Indian convicts sent by the British, who were given the choice to stay once they'd served their time. Many did that and were later joined by Indian labourers in search of work. These early labourers built hospitals and other essential buildings – and temples. Including, in 1855, the beautiful – though hard to pronounce – **Sri Veeramakaliamman Temple (141 Serangoon Road, 8am-12:30pm, 2pm-8.30pm, daily)**, a feature of Little India you **absolutely shouldn't miss.** It's on Serangoon Road, the main drag of Little India, which also encompasses Racecourse and Northumberland Roads, as well as Jalan Besar. The enclave is served by the Farrer Park, Rochor and Little India MRT stations; geographically, as the crow flies, it's **not far from the CBD.**

As well as this Hindu temple, which has an impressively colourful facade, atmospheric, smoke-filled interior and an intense aura of devotion, there are a few other sights in Little India. The **Mustafa Centre (145 Syed Alwi Road, 24 hours, daily)** is an everything-under-one-roof shopping institution that has to be experienced to be believed. On weekends, immigrant workers swarm to stock up on everything from toiletries, electronics and textiles to homewares and clothing. You can even buy gold wedding jewels. Sprawling and head-spinning, there's nowhere quite like it. The **Little India Arcade (48 Serangoon Road, various opening times)** is modest in comparison but a great place to pick up the scents of spice, a bag of *barfi*, some Hindi soundtracks, pictures of Lord Krishna, and get your hand hennaed. Last but not least, there's the **Tekka Centre food market and shops (Bukit Timah Road, 6.30am-9pm, daily)**, named after the old-time name for Little India and right by a Little India MRT exit. This is one of **Singapore's most colourful wet markets** and hawker centres ▷

79

– it's riotous. The offerings are predominantly, but not exclusively, Indian. After refuelling on *chapatis, biryani* and a glass of hot *teh tarik* (milky "pulled" tea), head upstairs for sari silks, Bollywood recordings and other exotic bits and bobs. Nearby **Buffalo Road is a good place to amble**, with its cheek-by-jowl produce and dry goods stores, garland sellers and bustling atmosphere. The impressive, four-storey **Indian Heritage Centre (5 Campbell Lane, 10am-7pm, closed Mon)** opened just a few years ago. A repository of artefacts, displays and galleries employing augmented reality, this modern museum paints the history and culture of Singapore's Indians in all their wondrous colour.

Kampong Glam, a five-minute walk from the Bugis MRT, is a tad more manicured. The vibe is **genteel and charming**, especially along the palm-fringed, pedestrianised Bussorah Street that strikes through its middle. At the end of Bussorah stands the imposing **Sultan Mosque (3 Muscat Street, 9am-1pm, 2pm-4pm, daily)**, with its **dazzling golden dome and soaring minarets**. Its beautiful interior can accommodate 5000 devotees. Dating from 1826, it's a vibrant place of worship and teaching.

Before British colonisation in 1819, Kampong Glam (whose name derives from *kampong* for 'village' and *glam*, from the Malay *gelam*, a type of paperbark tree) was the **seat of the ruling Malay aristocracy**. Under the 1822 Raffles Plan, whereby the city was sectioned into ethnic areas, Kampong Glam was designated Malay and Arab and many from these communities were merchants. While the cultural mix here expanded over time, the **area still has a relentlessly Arab and Malay Muslim flavour**. Shops selling Qurans and other Islamic paraphernalia, Muslim fashion, Persian carpets, oriental perfume and exotic textiles proliferate, particularly down the aptly named Arab Street. The **muezzin's call to prayer infuses the airwaves** and a conservative dress code, with many women covered, is the norm. But it's not all piety and pillars of faith around here. **Haji Lane**, a narrow walking street lined with **quaint old shophouses**, has been remade into a shopping/drinking precinct that attracts **the beau monde in their selfie-taking hordes**. The strip is a known bar-hopping destination and its cafes are draped with **studiously fashionable millennials**.

The **Malay Heritage Centre (85 Sultan Gate, 1pm-6pm Mon, 10am-6pm Tue-Sun)** is located in the old Sultan's palace, the Istana Kampong Glam. Here, 10 galleries, housed in a gorgeous old colonial building, paint a fascinating picture of the festivals, religious customs and aspirations of the largest ethnic group in Singapore. It's definitely worth some time.

Food is a real highlight of both these little pockets, with plenty of excellent cafes, restaurants and other outlets. It's mandatory to visit each area hungry. Very. ◆

The Sultan Mosque

At Rumah Makan Minang

Famous Haji Lane

Fragrance shop, Kampong Glam

TANDOORI CHICKEN
AND NAAN BREAD,
LITTLE INDIA

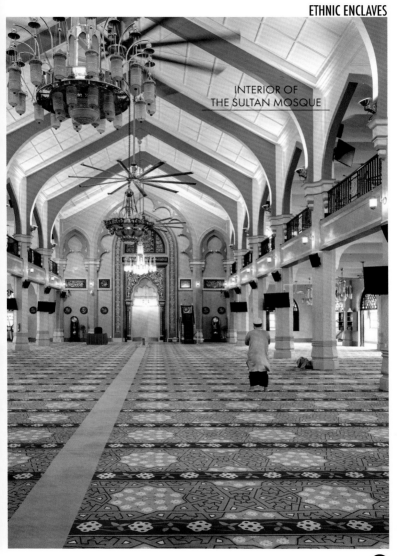

INTERIOR OF
THE SULTAN MOSQUE

ETHNIC ENCLAVES

The Curry Culture

WHERE TO EAT
Little India

THE CURRY CULTURE
12 Farrer Park Station Road.
11.45am-2.30pm, 5.30pm-10.30pm, daily
An offshoot of smart The Curry Culture at 31 Cuppage Road, the fare is as excellent as the surrounds, with an emphasis on modern presentation and smooth service. Dishes will take you on a culinary escapade – *machli amritsari* (fish fried in a spicy batter with mint sauce), *keema mattar* (minced lamb with peas and cardamom), and *kesari phirni*, a rice, cream and milk dessert, for starters.

MUSTARD
32 Racecourse Road.
11.30am-3pm, 6pm-10.45pm Sun-Fri
Specialising in Punjabi and Bengali fare, this airy place is away from the usual Little India hubbub. The authentic vegetarian snacks are particularly intriguing and the menu, supported by a wine list (praise be), is divided into useful categories like Clay 'n' Coal, Curry Trail and Farmer's Favourites.

AZMI RESTAURANT
166 Serangoon Road.
9am-10pm, daily
Nondescript? Yes. But oh, those chapatis – everyone says they're the best in town. The smell of toasty flour from flatbreads cooking, hits before you even see the place. Service can be scowly but for freshness, flavour and hobnobbing with the locals, you won't do better.

KOMALA VILAS
76/78 Serangoon Road.
7am-10.30pm, daily
Opened in 1947, south Indian vegetarian is the specialty, with a number of outlets citywide. The menu is good value with vegetarian *biryani*, south Indian *thali*, *chapati* and *dosai* among the favourites. Breakfast, lunch or dinner, this is a dependable, cheap bet.

KEBABS 'N CURRIES
L/7 Mustafa Centre, 171 Syed Alwi Road.
11am-12.45pm, daily
Atop the bustling Mustafa Centre and popular with large groups, this is a good place to find respite from the frenetic streets. The expansive à la carte menu, offering all the favs (butter chicken, *kebab*, *korma*, *biryani*, *naan* breads etc) is better than the curry buffet.

KHANSAMA TANDOORI
166 Serangoon Road.
11am-12.30am, daily
Unmissable, with its prominent corner location; there are outdoor tables. As the name suggests, tandoori dishes are what you should order; everything from pomfret, prawns, chicken, mutton, paneer and vegetables go though the oven's searing heat.

MAVALLI TIFFIN ROOMS
438 Serangoon Road.
8.30am-3pm, 5.30pm-
9.30pm Tues-Sun
Established in 1923, these guys are The Last Word in southern Indian comfort fare. Menu favs include the *rava idli* (steamed semolina cakes with cashews, curry leaves, coriander and mustard seeds), which they invented during WWII. And *kesari bhath*, a thick, sweet, saffron-infused semolina pudding. Staff, though busy, manage to remain charming.

Kampong Glam
Because they're halal, places here won't serve any alcohol.

KAMPONG GLAM CAFE
17 Bussorah Street.
8am-2am, daily
In the midst of the Kampong Glam action, this landmark place has been around since 2004. Join the queue (it's self-service) for *nasi padang* (a Sumatran dish of steamed rice with a selection of lively sides), and Malay/Indonesian staples like *mee rebus* (noodles in sweet potato gravy), *tahu goreng* (fried tofu with thick sweet-sour sauce), *soto ayam* (chicken noodle soup) and *gado gado* (vegetables, *tempeh* and boiled egg in spiced peanut sauce).

PADI@BUSSORAH
53 Bussorah Street.
6pm-9pm, daily
It's more expensive than other Malay/Indonesian options in this 'hood but it's more chic too; it's also within cooee of the glorious Sultan Mosque. They're known for delicious *nasi ambeng*, a Javanese specialty of rice with side dishes like curry, *sambal* squid, salted fish and fried coconut; theirs comes with up to 13 sides. You order by the platter size, depending on how many are dining.

ZAM ZAM
697-699 North Bridge Road.
7am-11pm, daily
Since 1908 they've been flippin' and fryin' their legendarily fat *murtabak*, a close cousin of *roti prata* (see pg 18). These are stuffed with combinations of minced meat (mutton, chicken, deer, beef or sardine), egg, onion and other vegetables, the mixture bolstered with a layer of cooked, torn *roti* dough. Folded into a square, they're cooked to crispness in copious oil and served with a side of curry gravy. Right across from the Sultan Mosque, the place isn't much to look at but the *murtabak*, which you can watch being made in the front window, is one of the best things you'll eat in Singapore.

WARONG NASI PARIAMAN
736-738 North Bridge Road.
7.30am-8pm, daily
This is the oldest *nasi padang* place in Singapore. Friday is madness here –

after prayers at the mosque, hundreds file through for specialties such as *ayam bakar* (barbecued chicken in an aromatic coconut gravy), beef *rendang* and *bagadel*, which are fried spheres of meaty, spiced mashed potato.

MIHRIMAH RESTAURANT
742 North Bridge Road.
7.30am-12am, daily
Earthy food direct from a Malay/Indonesian village is what to expect – *epok epok* (curry puffs), *tahu telur* (eggs, tofu and veg with prawn paste), oxtail soup and *siput sedut* (sea snails in coconut milk). Out the front, they make *roti prata* (see pg 18) and there's always a selection of local cakes hovering around, for the sweet toothed. Popular with families, it's incredibly affordable and very friendly.

RUMAH MAKAN MINANG
18 Kandahar Street.
8.30am-7.30pm, daily
Don't be fooled by the modern vibe – this friendly, but frenetic joint has been going since 1954. Another *nasi padang* place, just point to what you want from the selection and, if you get confounded by the choice, nice staff will help you out. The *rendang* is astoundingly good, the recipe passed down from the family's grandma. The *ikan bakar* (grilled fish), in sweet soy and chilli, is ripper too.

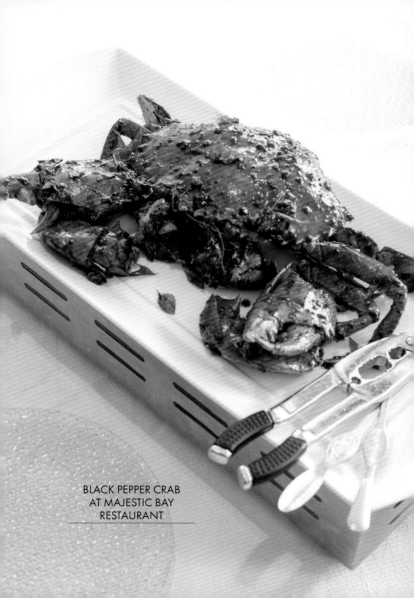

BLACK PEPPER CRAB
AT MAJESTIC BAY
RESTAURANT

If you never thought a crab could be better than its usual, sweet-fleshed self, it's time for a revelation or two. No one, but no one, cooks crab like a Singaporean and as for eating them, the locals are fiends. Give them a pile of cut-up crustacean and they'll sit and pick those suckers completely clean.

CRAB

Another contender for 'national dish' title, the history of Singaporean chilli crab is relatively short. It was only in 1956 that a street cooking couple decided to tinker with their crab dishes and branch out from the usual steamed formula. Madam Cher Yam Tian was the wife's name and at first, she simply stir-fried her crab with tomato sauce, before deciding it needed some chilli sauce too. This combo took off and was later tweaked by a restaurant chef, who used *sambal*, tomato paste, sugar and beaten egg, which cooked to fine threads in the gravy. This version is the basis for the standard that's served in Singapore today. (The story of Singapore crab gets up some Malaysian noses no end, actually. They contend THEY created the dish and ... oh, whatever, just don't mix your crab eating with national rivalries and politics; it could get messy.)

The sauce is thick, sweet, slightly spicy and very, very satisfying. You eat ▷

CRAB

the crab with *mantou*, or steamed Chinese buns, to mop up the sauce and, in the process, things do get a bit dribbly. You use crab crackers, metal pickers and your fingers to extract as much of the flesh as possible; most places provide a disposable bib to wear which, while no fashion statement, does a great job of protecting your clothes from stains. Meaty mud crabs, mainly imported from Sri Lanka, are the norm for this dish but there are various other species at play and what's available depends on the restaurant and the season. Crabs come from as far afield as Scotland and Alaska. Whichever type of crab you choose, you pay according to the weight, and good places will have them live in tanks, ensuring scrupulous freshness. The best way to cook them is to boil them first then finish them in the wok with the sauce, as this prevents the meat sticking to the shell, apparently.

Chilli crab at New Ubin

Just as popular as chilli crab is black pepper crab, invented in the 1950s too, at Long Beach restaurant. It's a drier affair than chilli crab, with none of that saucy gloop. Instead, the cracked crabby bits are wok-fried with butter, dried shrimp, curry leaves, fresh chilli, garlic, soy sauce and copious ground black pepper. There's also a white pepper version of this dish, found most famously on the menu of No Signboard Seafood (see pg 91), held to be the inventor. ◆

Black pepper crab at New Ubin

No Signboard Seafood Restaurant

FOOD & DRINKS

Other crab dishes

BUTTER CRAB

This is a Kuala Lumpur invention, but it's popular here and for good reason — that sauce (evaporated milk, butter, curry leaves and chilli) is delicious.

COFFEE CRAB

Yeah, really. The idea isn't new — there's a *zi char* dish of pork ribs in thick, sweet, tasty coffee sauce. But crab is novel. It was created at the Majestic Bay Restaurant (see pg 91) and involves wok frying crab with three types of coffee bean, apple jam, rice wine and butter, the whole thing flambéed in liquor before serving.

SALTED EGG YOLK CRAB

Salted egg yolk (from eggs treated with a salty brine that 'cooks' the egg — yolks become firm, crumbly and almost cheese like) was a big craze that settled into the culinary woodwork. You can literally get salted egg anything — steamed buns, ice-cream sauce and choux puffs, for example. It's also paired with crab; crab pieces are fried with chilli, curry leaves, mashed salted yolk and tons of butter.

TEOCHEW COLD CRAB

Carefully boiled, cooled then served on ice with a soy sauce and vinegar dip, this sounds simple, right? Not so fast. The secret is in getting male crabs right on the cusp of moulting, and ones that are full of milt (or sperm).

CRAB BEE HOON

Bee hoon (rice vermicelli) are ace at absorbing flavours. Crabs are cooked with them and seafood stock in two styles — a 'dry' one, where the gravy is thick and the flavours concentrated, and a claypot soup version. That soup can be simple or involve as many as 20 ingredients — adding evaporated milk, for a creamy edge, is the norm.

CHILLI CRAB READY
TO EAT AT J65

WHERE TO EAT

J65
1/F Hotel Jen Tanglin,
1A Cuscaden Road.
6.30am-11pm, daily
A great chilli crab can be had at this excellent hotel dining room, not far from Orchard Road. But, that buffet! On Wednesdays, Fridays and Saturdays they pile the ice high and top it with all manner of cooked seafood goodness, crabs included. Then there's the hot food stations where dishes steam away and entice, including chilli crab.

NO SIGNBOARD SEAFOOD RESTAURANT
414 Geylang Road.
11.30am-1.30am, daily
Dial the chilli quotient up, (or down) when you order at this legendary place; you chose how hot you want things. From humble beginnings as a food stall, to a constantly packed mega-restaurant, they're also the inventors of white pepper crab. Punters clamour for their chilli crab in particular, which arrives swimming in voluptuous sweet-savoury sauce. Many claim it's the best in town.

NEW UBIN SEAFOOD
L6/63 Hillview Avenue.
11.30am-10am, daily
This place has a long heritage, back to simple beginnings on the island of Pulau Ubin. Now they've several mainland outlets and this one is fantastic, with its canteen-style, open-

air vibe; it's tucked in the back of a carpark building. Granted, it's a touch hard to find but do NOT let that deter. The home-style cooking, including a stupendous chilli crab, black pepper crab and other seafood delights, is just great.

MAJESTIC BAY RESTAURANT
01-10, 18 Marina Gardens Drive.
11am-3pm, 5.45pm-9pm, daily
Combine a visit to the jaw-dropping Gardens By The Bay with a meal here. The chic dining room is beautifully light and airy, and the menu's a mix of traditional and contemporary seafood (and other) dishes. You HAVE to try the unique coffee crab; the chef advises that a 1.4kg mud crab is the optimum size to cook for the best flavour.

SIN HUAT EATING HOUSE
659 Lorong 35 Geylang.
6.30pm-1am, daily
The chef at this low-key, neighbourhood eatery is credited with inventing crab *bee hoon* and it's a cracking dish. But load up on cash before you come as Sin Huat is infamously pricey. There's no menu as such so you need to confirm the crab (and other seafood) prices before you order anything. Chef Danny chats you through the daily options before scurrying away to

cook – a couple of Aunties deliver food to the table. This place was famously visited by the late Anthony Bourdain who loved it.

JUMBO SEAFOOD
#B1-48, 20 Upper Circular Road.
12pm-3pm, 6pm-12am, daily
There are five outlets; this one is very handy to the CBD and the outlook, over the Singapore River, is lovely. There's outdoor seating to best soak in the views although the classy, cool interior is hardly a shabby option. Their chilli crab, which isn't overly spicy, has won 'Best In Singapore' awards in years past and the black pepper one is jolly decent too.

LONG BEACH@ DEMPSEY SEAFOOD RESTAURANT
25 Dempsey Road (via Holland Road).
1am-3pm, 5pm-1am, daily
Fish tanks gurgle and happy punters feast on the freshest crabs, scallops and other sea creatures here. Long Beach has come a long way since opening with just a few menu items in 1946 when, in the aftermath of WWII, Singaporeans rarely ate out. As well as being credited with the invention of black pepper crab, they also claim they introduced the concept of serving live seafood in restaurants to Singapore. Note: there are a few outlets of this place.

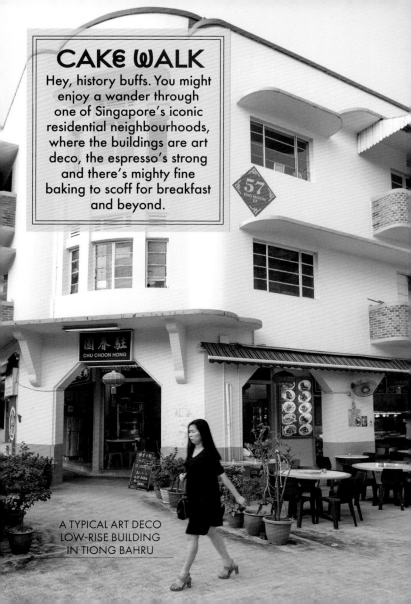

CAKE WALK

Hey, history buffs. You might enjoy a wander through one of Singapore's iconic residential neighbourhoods, where the buildings are art deco, the espresso's strong and there's mighty fine baking to scoff for breakfast and beyond.

A TYPICAL ART DECO LOW-RISE BUILDING IN TIONG BAHRU

We're talking Tiong Bahru. Here, heady nostalgia meets indie bookstores, niche boutiques, expat yummy mums and restful green spaces; the Modernist digs provide rich fodder for Instagrammers.

Pastries, Tiong Bahru Bakery

Built more than 80 years ago as a way to decrease overcrowding in nearby Chinatown, Tiong Bahru was the first public housing estate in Singapore. The original monthly rentals here were beyond the means of ordinary Singaporeans but not the rich, who used the flats to house their mistresses. As a result the precinct earned the titles 'mistress village' and 'den of beauties'. Its actual name means 'new cemetery' and there was indeed a Peranakan graveyard on this site until the 1920s.

There are 20 two-to five-storey apartment blocks left; these form the heritage precinct declared in 2003, and thank goodness for that. Things move and develop swiftly in Singapore and unprotected old structures are the first to go when space is needed. Pockets of quaint shophouses and other colonial-era buildings notwithstanding, Singapore can feel relentlessly new. But not so here, where the long, clear, cruise liner-like features of 1930s architecture fuse with elements of the local, so-called Nanyang Style. Porthole windows, rounded balconies, flat roofs and geometric precision are the Streamline Moderne hallmarks; the incorporation of shophouses, the use ▷

Barista on the job

TIONG BAHRU

of air wells and vents for cooling, and the external spiral staircases are elements of local architecture that were employed with tropical living in mind.

Just a 10-minute drive from the crowded hustle and buzz of the CBD, Tiong Bahru exudes a spacious, quiet air. Streets are named after rubber barons, merchants and other Chinese pioneers of the 19th and early 20th century, who made an impact on the city. Buildings are laid out, grid-like, around swathes of green lawn, with plenty of palms doing a gentle sway. Today's inhabitants are a mix of expats, hip young things and a smattering of old-timers. There's some fascinating history. For example, the block at 78 Guan Chuan Street still has air-raid shelters and storage rooms used during WWII. Nelson's Tailor, in Block 58 on Seng Poh Road, made the first Singapore Airlines uniforms, to Pierre Balmain designs, in the early 1970s. Pin Pin Piau Kay & Co, a minimart in Block 71 on Seng Poh Road, has been in business since 1938 and is still run by the same family.

Today, the government is putting the brakes on Tiong Bahru morphing into a groovy retail enclave; some businesses in lower floor apartments have been forced out so the spaces can be returned to their original purpose – apartment living. ◆

Drips Bakery Cafe

Breakfast at Merci Marcel

Incense holder

Street art decorates Tiong Bahru

Typical apartment exterior

Berry-topped cheesecake at Drips

Cheng's pandan chiffon cake

Covered walkways are a feature

Merci Marcel

Butterfly cakes from Galicier Bakery

WHERE TO CAFFEINATE

TIONG BAHRU BAKERY
#01-70, 56 Eng Hoon
Street.
8am-8pm, daily
An artisan bakery that pumps from morning to night. Their buttery croissants, ham-filled baguettes, sandwiches in squid ink buns, chocolate tarts and mixed berry crumble are best eaten with a cup of the excellent coffee, courtesy of skilled baristas and Common Man Coffee Roasters beans.

DRIPS BAKERY CAFE
#01-05, 82 Tiong Poh
Road.
11am-9.30pm Sun-Thurs,
11am-11pm Fri-Sat
Score an outside table and pretend you live here. Drips is an adored local, slightly out of the main action. The cabinet selection of glazed fruit tarts, sugar-dusted berry-topped cheesecakes, buttery teacakes and crumbly cookies will have you salivating.

FORTY HANDS
#01-12, 78 Yong Siak
Street.
7am-7pm, daily
When espresso culture exploded across Singapore around 2010, Forty Hands was one of the first to set benchmarks. They use Common Man Coffee Roasters' beans, a premium local brand, and their baristas are knowledgeable. The daytime menu runs the gamut of eggs *en cocotte*, house-made granola and banana bacon french toast. Perch inside the hip but homey room at the skinny bar, or in the cute courtyard.

WHISK CAFE
58 Seng Poh Road.
9am-7pm (closed Mon)
The owner interned at Dominique Ansel's bakery in New York. No surprise then that the moreish carrot cakes, zesty lemon tarts and macarons are exemplary. They serve high tea in the afternoon (for a minimum of two), featuring their signature desserts, sandwiches, homemade scones and jam. Look for limited-edition specials like gin and tonic cupcakes made with Hendrick's gin.

GALICIER
55 Tiong Bahru Road.
10am-8.30pm (closed
Mon)
A long-time favourite, in the oldest block in Tiong Bahru, peddling a selection of Nyonya and other cakes and cookies. It's a bakery, not a cafe, so grab sweet treats to take away, including *kueh dar dar* (pandan and coconut crepes), *ondeh ondeh* (rice flour balls stuffed with *gula melaka*), steamed tapioca cake, cute *putu ayu* (steamed pandan and coconut cupcakes) and even butterfly cakes.

CHENG'S @ 27
27 Yong Siak Street.
10am-3pm, 5.30pm-
10pm (closed Tues)
Unofficially, pandan chiffon cake is Singapore's 'national cake' and debates constantly rage as to who makes the best. This family-run *zi char*-style place has food veering towards Hainanese. But the aroma of pandan cake baking is the big draw, made with quality *gula melaka* and extra virgin coconut oil.

PLAIN VANILLA BAKERY
1D Yong Siak Street.
8am-7pm, daily
They use the best ingredients (Madagascan vanilla, French butter, Valrhona chocolate etc) in their excellent baking, such as the salted caramel truffle tart and red velvet cupcakes. Sit in the minimalist airconned room, a favoured spot for laptop toilers, or under cover outside, at a communal table, where the dog owners congregate.

MERCI MARCEL
#01-68, 56 Eng Hoon
Street.
9am-11.30pm Tues-Fri,
8am-11.30pm Sat-Sun
A très Frenchy cafe/bistro/bar with an excellent cheese and wine selection. Lunch is brunchy, featuring great bakes (are these the best croissants in town, or what?), smoked salmon in a pretzel bun, brioche French toast topped with cherry-berry compote, Bayonne ham platter and eggs most ways. Coffee beans are from local specialist roaster Tiong Hoe Specialty Coffee and gee they're good .

Hell yeah … skewered sticks of meaty, smoky, juicy goodness, slathered in thick, peanut sauce and eaten with blocks of compressed rice. Satay is maybe Singapore's most iconic dish. An import from the Arabs via Java, its close association with the Lion City goes back to around 1940, so they reckon.

SATAY

Singaporeans, though, will tell you that good satay is becoming harder to find. Compared to The Glory Days, that is, when The Satay Club, a loose collection of satay stalls strung along Beach Road during the 1950s and 60s which later moved to Esplanade Park, reigned supreme. Here the coals were cranked up for grilling in the early evening so punters could eat al fresco; this informed the way satay is eaten in Singapore today. Although many hawker centres have satay outlets, dedicated, evening-focused hotspots remain popular and they include Satay By The Bay (see pg 101), a pleasant destination close to Gardens By The Bay. And the legendary Lau Pa Sat satay extravaganza, which sees the closing of traffic every evening along Boon Tat Street (see pg 101) in the CBD.

The most commonly used meats for satay are beef, mutton, lamb and chicken and, among non-Muslims, pork. Sometimes, you'll see duck on ▷

SATAY

offer. Thin dried stems of coconut leaf were originally used as sticks but these days, it's bamboo all the way. There are two styles of satay in Singapore – Chinese and Malay. Chinese satay sees the raw meat lightly infused with five-spice powder and threaded on sticks with alternating pieces of fat. Malay satay is marinated in ground, fragrant spices and aromatics like fennel, coriander, cumin, turmeric, garlic and ginger – the exact composition can change from cook to cook. Sometimes, lime leaves are used, or galangal, for example. Some cooks finish their peanut sauce with a swirl of *kecap manis* (thick, sweet soy sauce) for extra sweetness. The Malay version sees no extra fat threaded on the skewers. Finely chopped or pureed pineapple is sometimes added to the peanut dipping sauce. Either way, skewers are grilled over a charcoal fire, the heat controlled by cooks using a fan to encourage the flames. The meat is brushed regularly with oil, cooked until it's well browned then served with peanut sauce to dip and bits of cucumber and red onion. Plus there are cubes of *ketupat*, which are compressed, steamed rice wrapped in woven coconut-leaf packets before cooking.

Prawn satay is a relatively new iteration. *Satay bee hoon* was invented by Singaporean Teochew cooks, who cottoned on to the slathering of peanut sauce over rice vermicelli, cuttlefish, *kang kong*, beansprouts, pork slices, prawns or cockles, or a combination thereof. Yum. And 'satay'? Word is, the name comes from the Tamil for flesh, '*sathai*'. Not the Hokkien '*sar teh*' for 'three pieces'. Now you know. ◆

At Satay By The Bay

Packets of compressed rice

At Lau Pa Sat

WHERE TO EAT

SATAY BY THE BAY
18 Marina Gardens Drive.
11.30am-1am, daily
Satay By The Bay is what
happens when you take the
concept of a hawker centre
slightly upscale, plonking
it in calming greenery,
away from the city's push
and shove. There's a range
of hawker dishes on offer,
despite the specific name.
And, although the centre
opens at 11.30am, note
that the satay outlets (and
there are a few: Power
Satay, Warung Satay,
Huat Satay, Leo Satay, City
Satay, for example) don't
fire up until about 5pm. This
is an excellent place to dine
after a day at Gardens By
The Bay, right next door.

LAU PA SAT SATAY STREET
18 Raffles Quay.
7pm-1am Mon-Fri,
3pm-1am Sat-Sun
For many, Lau Pa Sat IS
satay in Singapore. It's
certainly popular with the
tourists who flock here
every night to chow down
on skewers of meat by the
heaving platterful. You
come for the smoke-filled,
party vibe as much as for
the food, which some local
experts dismiss as pretty
average. Which is maybe
a touch unfair. Stalls 7 and
8 really go off, with their
delicious sauce and crusty,
glistening beef, mutton,
chicken and prawn sticks.
Target the most popular

outlets for the tastiest
offerings, grab a beer and
sit at an outdoor table for
the best experience.

KWONG SATAY
549 Geylang Road.
5pm-11pm, daily
It looks unprepossessing in
its dowdy *kopi tiam* setting
in Geylang, but stick with
it. These guys are super
nice, their satay is super
delicious and those in the
know say it's because they
put a dash of saffron in
their marinade, along with
around 18 other spices.
The *pièce de résistance*
here is the charming
owner's special creation
– pork belly satay. You
heard right –Pork. Belly.
Satay. It's incredible.

HARON 30 SATAY
Stall 55, East Coast
Lagoon Food Village,
1220 East Coast Parkway.
3pm-11pm Tues-Fri,
12pm-11pm Sat-Sun
This food centre is fantastic,
with its al fresco beachside
setting. There are a few
satay outlets in the mix,
which crank up late in the
afternoon and grill into the
evening. The chicken satay
from Haron, with its sturdy,
flavoursome chunks of
bird meat and homemade
peanut sauce, is tops. They
also do mutton, beef and
awesome wings, too. The
daughters of the original
owner have now taken
over the business.

VIOLET OON SATAY BAR & GRILL
3B River Valley Road,
#01-18 Clarke Quay.
6pm-12am, daily
Violet Oon is considered
Singapore's national food
ambassador and is a local
culinary legend. She lends
her expertise to a few
outlets around town and this
one, as the name suggests,
is All About The Satay
(though there are plenty
of other delicious bites on
the menu too). Choose
from chicken, prawn, beef,
pork or even tripe satay;
the emphasis is on high-
quality meats, which can't
necessarily be said of other
satay places. Homemade
marinades and the spicy
peanut sauce are divine.

CHUAN KEE SATAY
#01-85, 51 Old Airport
Road.
6pm-10pm (closed Mon
and Thurs)
Singaporean foodies highly
rate this place, known
for its especially fragrant,
succulent Chinese-style satay
which, they claim, blows
any competition out of the
water. Judge for yourself
but know that at busy times,
you may have to wait up to
45 minutes for food. At least
you're at one of the best food
centres in the city (see pg 52)
so can readily quell those
hunger pangs while you
wait. You order a minimum of
10 sticks and you'll want to
eat at least that many.

Peranakan Singapore

Despite Singapore's pristine modernity, there's plenty of material evidence of its striking Peranakan heritage. 'Peranakan' refers to those of mixed Chinese and Malay (or Indonesian) blood; they trace their origins back to the 15th century, when Chinese traders intermarried with local women.

GRILLED SNAPPER
AT CANDLENUT

THE NATIONAL
KITCHEN BY
VIOLET OON

PERANAKAN SINGAPORE

Traditional beaded shoes

Ayam buah keluak at Straits Kitchen

Peranakan porcelain

Embroidered jacket at Rumah Bebe

Peranakans are also referred to as the 'Straits Chinese', because their main concentrations were in Singapore, Penang and Malacca, all in the Straits of Malacca. You'll also hear them called 'Baba Nyonyas'. The Babas are the men of the group and the Nyonyas the women; their cuisine is commonly referred to as 'Nyonya'.

This unique, hybrid culture is a mix of Malay and Chinese and is evidenced in dress, architecture, crafts, language and cuisine. Generally, Peranakans were of the business class and considered somewhat elite. Many were British educated and fluent in several languages; they were known as the 'King's Chinese' for their loyalty to the British crown. Their own lingo (today spoken fluently by fewer than 1000 in Singapore) is a Malay patois, adulterated with liberal sprinklings of Hokkien words and phrases.

Nyonya food is highly refined; culinary skills were (and still are) prized. It was unthinkable for a prospective Nyonya bride to not be an excellent cook. She was also expected to be accomplished in the fine embroidery and beadwork that were such a distinctive feature of Peranakan dress and home decor.

In their cooking, a blend of Chinese and local Malay elements have given rise to unique dishes that are at once tangy, aromatic, spicy, rich and herbal. Fragrant dishes like *assam* (tamarind) fish, beef *rendang*, *jiu hu char* (finely shredded carrot, daikon radish, mushroom, pork and cuttlefish eaten in lettuce leaves as a hand-held wrap) and *ayam buah keluak* (chicken cooked in thick sauce that's dark with tamarind and a meaty, black nut called *buah keluak*), are typical. *Kueh pie tee* (see pg 106) and even *laksa* had their origins with the Nyonyas. *Belacan* (fermented shrimp paste) is an essential ingredient and fresh aromatics (lemongrass, kaffir lime, chilli, turmeric etc), dry spices (cumin, cinnamon, fennel seed, five spice etc) and coconut milk are widely used. Pork is enjoyed, marking a departure from halal Malay cooking. *Kueh*, in dazzling colours and myriad shapes (see pg 114), are another distinctive feature.

Nyonya dishes rely on the painstaking grinding of spices and hand-pounding of foundational spice pastes, using a mortar and pestle. Recipes tended not to be written down but were interpreted differently from one cook to another; kitchens guarded their secrets jealously. There are a number of authentic Nyonya restaurants and culinary experts in Singapore; the best restaurants are family run, using recipes passed down generations. In the old suburb of Joo Chiat, near Katong, there are rows of heritage Peranakan homes with their elaborate facades and eye-catching colours. A visit to the **Peranakan Museum (39 Armenian Street, 10am-7pm, daily)** is highly recommended. ▷

Some typical Nyonya dishes

Acar awak: a vegetable pickle (using snake beans, carrot, cucumber etc) cooked using vinegar, palm sugar, ginger, turmeric and other spices

Acar ikan: small fried fish marinated in oil, tamarind, and garlic

Asam pedas: a sour fish curry cooked with pineapple

Ayam buah keluak: chicken cooked with the pulp of a native Indonesian black nut, *buah keluak*. The pulp is toxic if the nut isn't soaked and fermented first. It's then ground into a paste with candlenuts, turmeric, galangal, lemon grass, *belacan* and dried chilli, and made into a stew with the chicken

Babi pongteh: sweet-salty braised pork belly flavoured with *tau cheo* (fermented soy beans), soy sauce and with *gula melaka* (palm sugar)

Bubur cha cha: a dessert featuring chunks of taro, sweet potato, banana and sago in coconut milk; variations, such as the addition of durian, are common

Chap chye: a mixed vegetable stir-fry given a pungent, salty edge with the addition of *tau cheo* (fermented soy beans)

Inchi kabin: spice-marinated chicken pieces that are deep-fried

Itek tim: a comfort-food soup of salted vegetables, duck, tomatoes, tamarind juice, tamarind skins and chilli

Jiu hu char: cooked shreds of carrot, mushroom and daikon radish with shredded cuttlefish and pork, eaten wrapped in lettuce leaves

Kueh pie tee: a wholly Pernankan invention; a delicate, crisp, fried and fluted batter case, formed using a special mould, is filled with a finely shredded vegetable and prawn mixture. Flavours are sweet and spicy

Nasi kunyit: glutinous rice cooked with coconut milk and stained yellow with turmeric. Served with *rendang*, curries and other spicy dishes

Ngoh hiang: literally 'five fragrances'. Minced pork, infused with five spice powder, is rolled in beancurd skin to form a neat round package, then deep-fried. Served in slices with plum sauce to dip

Sambal udang petai: also found in Malay and Indonesian cuisines, a dish of prawns and bright green, sightly bitter 'stink' beans (*petai*) stir-fried in a rich, smoky chilli paste

Satay babi sum chan: a pork belly stew whose prominent flavours are coconut and lemongrass

Udang masak nanas: prawns cooked in a coconutty curry with plenty of spices and slightly underripe pineapple

OLD PERANAKAN
HOUSES IN
JOO CHIAT

Dry Nyonya *laksa* at Rumah Bebe

Violet Oon's tapioca cake

Classic *kueh pie tee*

Lanterns at Rumah Bebe

WHERE TO EAT

RUMAH BEBE
113 East Coast Road.
9.30am-6.30pm Tues-Sun
This place is a trove.
Owner Bebe Seet isn't just
an astoundingly polished
Peranakan cook, she also
teaches the dying craft of
Nyonya beading in her
atelier upstairs. You can buy
her beaded shoes and bags,
all painstakingly worked
by hand. Wonderful. But
back to that food. Everything
served from the daily menu is
made from scratch, using all-
natural ingredients. The food
is mainly for taking away but
on the weekend you can eat
around her six-seater table if
you're organised enough to
book; demand is high.

BABA CHEWS BAR AND EATERY
#01-01 Katong Square,
86 East Coast Road.
6.30am-11pm Mon-Thurs,
6.30am-12am Fri-Sat
This is the diner for the
modish Hotel Indigo,
and things can get a little
fusionish here. So prepare
for black *buah keluak* on
your burger. And for the
lah milo, their Singaporised
take on Italian tiramisu. The
menu fully shines when the
chefs deliver the classics:
the memorable short rib
rendang, pong tauhu (a
Peranakan soup made with
homemade prawn stock and
pork meatballs), and *telur
dadar cincalok*, omelette
spiked with a Nyonya
fermented prawn condiment.

BLUE GINGER
97 Tanjong Pagar Road.
12pm-2.30pm, 6.30pm-
10.30pm, daily
Something of an institution,
this polished and popular
restaurant is in a moody,
simply decorated old
shophouse. Try to score
a seat on the upstairs
verandah, then tuck into
well-executed signatures
such as *pie tee, itek tim*, beef
rendang, cendol and *gula
melaka* (sago pudding with
palm sugar).

THE NATIONAL KITCHEN BY VIOLET OON
1 St Andrew's Road,
#02-01 National Gallery
Singapore.
12am-2.30am, 3pm-5pm,
6pm-10.30pm, daily
She departs from tradition
– using *buah keluak* on
spaghetti, for example – but
Violet Oon is a national
culinary treasure (see pg
101) and her gorgeous
restaurant, with its pendant
chandeliers and striking tiled
floors, is on its way to treasure
status too. Not all dishes
are Peranakan but plenty
are – *chap chye, jiu hu char,
assam* fish and *buah keluak
ayam*, for example. Visit the
amazing National Gallery
before or after dining.

CANDLENUT
Block 17A, Dempsey Road.
12pm-3pm, 6pm-10pm
Sun-Thurs,
12pm-3pm, 6pm-11pm,
Fri-Sat
Worth the trip up Dempsey
Hill, where historic army
barracks have been

PERANAKAN SINGAPORE
converted into a dining/
shopping precinct of the
loveliest kind. Never mind
that modern Candlenut has a
Michelin star! Go the tasting
menu route – you can leave
it to the chef to decide.
Beautiful presentation and
lively flavours are the
hallmarks of dishes like
coconut crab curry, *pie tee*,
tiger prawns with *sambal*,
and red snapper with green
mango and ginger flower.

STRAITS KITCHEN
Grand Hyatt Singapore,
10 Scotts Road.
12pm-2.30pm, 6.30pm-
10.30pm Mon-Fri,
12.30pm-3pm, 6.30pm-
10.30pm Sat-Sun
Yes they serve their fare
buffet-style and if you're not
a fan of that, relax. Hyatt do
it very damned well. Dishes
run the entire local gamut
(Indian, Malay, Chinese)
and the Peranakan selection
is comprehensive. The hotel
actually employs top hawker
cooks to deliver the most
authentic, local flavours.

CHONG WEN GE CAFE
168 Telok Ayer Street.
10am-7pm, daily
In a courtyard of the
visit-worthy Thian Hock
Keng Temple, right near the
Peranakan Tiles Gallery, this
cafe was started as a way
to show new generations
Singapore's culinary roots.
The interior is charming and
the Nyonya food affordable,
with their signature *satay bee
hoon*, with cuttlefish, clams,
kang kong and pig's liver,
clocking in at under $10.

ROASTED CHICKEN
AT GOOD YEAR
CHICKEN RICE BALL

To open a real hornet's nest, ask some Singaporeans where the best chicken rice is. The type of chicken, the fluffiness of the rice, the freshness of the sauce, the flavour of the poaching liquid, the way the chook's cut, the texture of the skin ... they're all up for contention.

CHICKEN RICE

It's a complicated, and crucial, question. After all, chicken rice (or Hainanese chicken rice to be precise) is believed by many to be the national dish here, despite other contenders and the fact it's also cooked in other parts of South-East Asia. And, in 2011, it made the vaunted CNN list of the world's 50 most delicious foods, coming in at number 45. It's ubiquitous – you'll see whole, pale, cooked birds hanging from hawker stalls everywhere, ready to eat. It also appears on many restaurant menus, from the humble to the haute and through to the franchised. The chicken is prepared by a gentle poaching in sub-boiling water, then it's shocked in iced water to quickly arrest the cooking, lock in all the juices and firm the flesh. The skin takes on an almost jelly-like consistency. This is a relatively modern touch – back in the day, the cooked chicken was simply cooled at room temperature, and rubbed with sesame oil. ▷

CHICKEN RICE

Artfully chopped into neat pieces through the bone, the chicken is served at room temperature with hot rice, a few slices of cucumber and a slick of chilli or soy sauce on the side for dipping. On paper, it almost sounds boring. In reality, it's anything but. This style of chicken rice originated on the southern Chinese island of Hainan where it developed as a way to deal with tasty, local birds called Wenchang chickens. Immigrants from that part of China introduced the dish to Singapore where today it's evolved to use tender, young chickens; the Hainanese preferred older birds with more fat.

Hainan chicken rice at a hawker centre

When properly cooked – and it is a skill – the flesh should be incredibly tender and succulent and a little pink around the bones. This method of cooking is from the Cantonese, celebrated for their *pak cham kai* or 'white cut chicken', cooked exactly this way and best suited to young, tender birds. The accompanying rice tastes particularly rich and fragrant; it's fried first in chicken fat then cooked in chicken stock with pandan leaf and slices of ginger. A bowl of chicken stock, sprinkled with a little green onion and chopped coriander, is served as part of the dish as a kind of light soup. There's an older version of chicken rice, seldom seen now, where the rice is served in compact balls, formed by hand. In this case the rice is shorter grained and somewhat heavier. It's also common to have the chicken braised with soy sauce or even roasted. ◆

The Most Famous Chicken Rice In Town!

Loy Kee Chicken Rice

WHERE TO EAT

TIAN TIAN HAINANESE CHICKEN RICE

1 Kadayanallur Street,
#01-10/11 Maxwell Food Centre.

10am-8pm (closed Mon)

It was famous before the late Anthony Bourdain visited but afterwards, the place went ballistic. Maybe the most famous chicken rice stall in the country, it's on every must-eat list in existence. It's now run by the owner's daughter, who gave up accountancy to expand the brand (there are numerous outlets now). Their famous cooking sauce brings earthy depth and you eat the chicken with hot rice and a trio of dipping sauces – chilli, dark soy and minced ginger.

TIONG BAHRU HAINANESE BONELESS CHICKEN RICE

#02-82 Tiong Bahru Market, 30 Seng Poh Road.

10am-8pm (closed Mon)

This is the original; there are a couple of other outlets, the most conveniently located of which is at 56 Smith Street, Chinatown. Along with Tian Tian, it's been included in the Michelin Bib Gourmand list. The owner learned his craft from a legendary hotel chef and has honed a subtle, less fatty, cleaner tasting bird, adding onion to his rice for added sweetness. He serves around 40 whole birds in a day and he closes once they're all gone.

LEONG YEOW FAMOUS WATERLOO ST CHICKEN RICE

#01-29 Nan Tai Eating House, 261 Waterloo Street.

10.30am-8.30pm, daily

The small hawker centre is great, with a fabulous location in Bras Basah. The white chicken is so tender and the roasted version is excellent too, with homemade garlic/chilli sauce. Queues can snake for ages at peak mealtimes.

CHICKEN HOUSE

#01-01 Kilat Court, 17 Lorong Kilat.

10.30am-8.30pm, daily

They're known for their flavoursome *kampong* (village) or free-range chicken, with yellow skin and lean, firm flesh. While it's not as plump as regular birds, aficionados do love their flavour and here, they're cooked with a little ginger for an aromatic edge.

GOOD YEAR CHICKEN RICE BALL

#01-366 Chang Cheng Mee Wah Coffee Shop, Block 111 Lorong 1, Toa Payoh.

10.30am-8pm (closed Fri)

They roll their rice into balls, kneading it into shape and mushing it slightly. The husband and wife owners both come from chicken rice-cooking families, going back to the 1940s. Located in a bustling neighbourhood hawker centre, it's popular. Those balls are large, BTW – two each is plenty.

SINN JI HAINANESE CHICKEN RICE

#01-05 Novena Regency, 275 Thomson Road.

11am-9pm, daily

This place is unusual as it's helmed by a hawker cook in his 20s, Derwin Chan, who left a career in animation to pursue his love of cooking. He's perfected a unique technique of inserting a custom-made metal tube into his birds to keep the water circulating inside, ensuring even cooking. He's so fussy he insists on Indonesian ginger, claiming the taste is more pungent.

LOY KEE CHICKEN RICE

342 Balestier Road.

10am-10pm, daily

Iconic Loy Kee has been around since 1953. The nostalgic interior is pleasant or you can sit at a table on the pavement. Order the Loy Kee Special Set, which includes vegetables as well as rice, soup and dipping sauces for the chicken. Ask for either roast or white-cooked chook; all served on a round wooden tray.

WEE NAM KEE,

#04-102B Marina Square, 6 Raffles Boulevard.

10.30am-9.30pm, daily

A *zi char* place with excellent home-style dishes, where locals love ordering a plate heaped with mixed chicken – half white-cooked, half roasted. The broth is ultra tasty, the rice exceptionally fluffy. There are a few other outlets; the original is at 101 Thomson Road.

A SELECTION
OF *KUEH*

From steamed to baked to wrapped in banana leaf and grilled, from striking blue to layered in gorgeous, multi-hued stripes, to topped with globs of *kaya* (egg and coconut jam), *kueh* are a revelation. A delicious snack, there's no right time to eat them. Breakfast, lunch or dinner – take your pick.

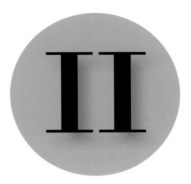

KUEH

Stand warned however, these little morsels are addictive. *Kueh* is a broad term that's taken to mean 'cakes', but it encompasses savoury as well as sweet snacks. Main ingredients include glutinous rice, rice, mung bean and tapioca flours (you will rarely encounter wheat flour) coconut milk, sago pearls and *gula melaka* (palm sugar). Pandan is used to flavour (and colour) *kueh* green, and banana leaves are often used as wrappers, before steaming. Savoury versions feature ingredients like taro, turnip, green vegetables, peanuts, chives and dried prawn. Both savoury and sweet *kueh* can be stained blue using butterfly pea flower. This tiny, intensely blue flower is a hallmark of Nyonya cooking in particular – the blooms are dried then steeped in hot water which, after a time, turns deep indigo. The water, which is largely tasteless, is strained then used for cooking, turning whatever it touches a stunning blue. ▷

KUEH

KUEH SALAT

A Nyonya *kueh* comprising a steamed pandan egg custard layer on top of a steamed glutinous rice base, the latter often marbled a natural blue using blue pea flower.

KUEH LOPES

Steamed, pandan-infused glutinous rice wrapped in a triangular shape in banana leaves. The cooked *kueh* are rolled in fresh, lightly salted grated coconut and served with *gula melaka* syrup.

KUEH BINGKA UBI

Baked tapioca cake. Made from grated tapioca (also called cassava), eggs, sugar, a little butter and coconut milk. The top is crusty and brown while the inside is soft and chewy.

HUAT KUEH

Soft, fluffy and not-too-sweet, these steamed cupcakes come in a whole range of colours. Different communities use different ingredients, some use wheaten cake flour while the Nyonya version is based on fermented sticky rice.

PNG KUEH

Pear-shaped, Teochew glutinous rice-flour cakes, formed in special moulds and usually tinted pink. The savoury filling involves glutinous rice, boiled peanuts, mushrooms and dried prawns.

KUEH DADAR

A fine green crepe coloured with pandan juice (food colouring is often used) rolled around a fresh grated coconut and *gula melaka* filling.

KEK LAPIS SARAWAK

Very labour-intensive to make, this is cooked, one thin layer of sponge cake mixture at a time, directly under a grill. The more skilled the baker, the more layers the cake has.

PULUT INTI

A pyramid-shaped Nyonya cake with a glutinous rice base that's marbled blue using butterfly pea flower. It is topped with grated coconut cooked with *gula melaka*; this mix is called '*inti*' or 'filling'. Traditionally they're wrapped in banana leaf to serve.

KUEH

KUEH LAPIS

A Nyonya classic – thin layers of different coloured tapioca flour/coconut milk batter are steamed, one layer at a time and on top of each other. Traditionally there are nine layers and the overall effect is gorgeously jewel-like.

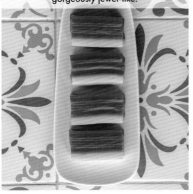

ONDEH ONDEH

Small rice-flour dumplings, tinted green with pandan juice, and stuffed with *gula melaka*. They're poached in water until cooked, then coated in freshly grated coconut.

REMPAH UDANG

A log of glutinous rice infused with coconut, filled with a savoury spiced dried prawn mixture, wrapped in banana leaf and steamed. Sometimes the rice is marbled with blue pea flower.

ANG KU KUEH

Formed in a special mould, the soft, sticky, red rice-flour skin encases a sweet filling of either peanut or mung bean. These originated in China, but the Nyonya version in Singapore is richer and more moist.

Whatever kueh are made from, you can expect pudding-like textures that run the gamut: thick and rich, smooth and light, soft and silky, chewy, fragrant, soothing, sweet, jellied, sticky or meltingly lush.

Kueh show Hokkien and Teochew Chinese or Malay influences, with many sorts associated with the Nyonyas (see pg 102). There's no definitive recipe for a particular type of kueh because traditionally they were made by the women of a house, who subscribed to a cooking method called 'agak agak', or 'approximation'. This relied on instinct and 'feel' as to how much of an ingredient to add, and for how long to cook each type of cake. Preparations can be time consuming; the old way involves freshly grinding/grating flours/coconut, and colours used were extracted from leaves, herbs and flowers. Making kaya jam (used to top certain kueh) from scratch, using coconut, egg and palm sugar, involves hours of vigilant stirring over low heat. Some kueh rely on processes that evolve over two or three days. ◆

WHERE TO EAT

POH CHEU SOON WAY
#01-230,127 Bukit Merah Lane 1.
8am-6pm Mon-Sat
A posse of cooks fashion kueh by hand the old-fash way. In business for 30 years, the third generation now run the show and are most noted for their variety of different flavoured ang ku kueh, with salted bean, durian, coffee, mango and green tea types, all different colours.

AH YEE'S SOON KUEH
124 Tembeling Road.
8am-5pm, daily
A small Teochew operation that's mainly takeaway; there are a couple of tables. Jeffrey Goh, the young owner, left his day job to help his mum carry on her business where absolutely everything is made fresh each day. Try the ku chye kueh, with its intense chive and dried prawn filling.

KIM CHOO KUEH CHANG
60 Joo Chiat Place.
9am-9pm, daily
This cake shop is as much a shrine to Peranakan culture (see pg 102) as it is a ripper place to buy traditional Nyonya-style kueh. While they're famous for their rice dumplings, the kueh selection is notable for its variety and freshness.

LEK LIM NYONYA CAKE CONFECTIONERY
#01-21, Blk 84 Bedok North Street 4.
4am-6pm Mon-Sat,
4am-2pm Sun
You need to be keen to venture to Bedok MRT then cab from there. But gee, the cakes! Lek Lim supplies hotels and the quality is brilliant. You'll find a few unusual gems, such as kotoh ubi, made from mashed tapioca and topped with lashings of caramelised coconut.

JI XIANG CONFECTIONERY
1 Everton Park.
8.30am-5pm Mon-Fri,
8am-5pm Sat
Spectacular handmade ang ku kueh, with a delicious, chewy rice-flour skin, is what punters queue for. The business started in 1985 with just two sorts (peanut and sweet bean), but now the line-up includes coconut, corn, yam and durian.

HARRIANN'S NYONYA TABLE
230 Victoria Street,
#01-01A, Bugis Junction Towers.
7am-9pm, daily
They offer their cakes with kopi, an unorthodox combo that works well. Try their famous ondeh ondeh, the kueh salat, with its kaya custard topping, or the pink fairy, a pretty pastel layering of coconut cream custard and adzuki bean.

Sling it back

A wine on a breezy rooftop, a cocktail in a sultry little bolthole or a beer with the best in a hotel bar… Singapore's drinking options are many and varied. Year round, the weather begs a cooling libation after sightseeing, shopping and scarfing down food. So when the clock chimes G+T o'clock, frock up and rock up to one of these brilliant destinations.

THE MARTINI BAR AT
THE GRAND HYATT
SINGAPORE

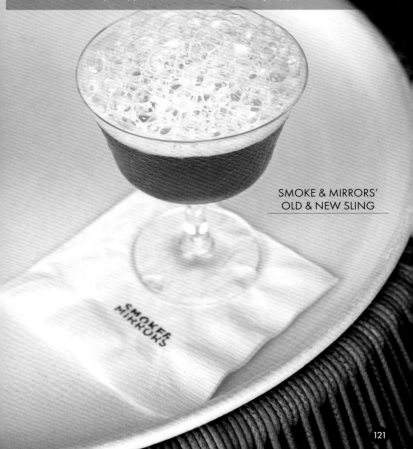

SMOKE & MIRRORS
#06-01 National Gallery Singapore, 1 St Andrew's Road. 3pm-1am Mon-Fri,
12pm-2am Sat-Sun

Wedged into a patio on the side of the National Gallery building, the al fresco seats are
the ones to nab, with their lovely outlook across to Marina Bay Sands. Right in front is
the Padang, a sports ground and, if you're lucky, there might be a bit of cricket going on.
Drinks-wise, it's Cleverly Crafted all the way, with a head bartender on something of a
creative mission. Take his rye whiskey-based Old & New Sling, for example, where the
surface is awash with pineapple bubbles, set into shape using soy protein.

SMOKE & MIRRORS'
OLD & NEW SLING

SINGAPORE SLING
AT RAFFLES HOTEL

SINGAPORE SLING

Ah, the Singapore Sling. It has to be done while you're in town – no? But if you'd prefer to save the SGD36.50 (at the time of writing) required to imbibe the city's iconic pink drink at the place of its invention (Raffles Hotel), then read on. Because we can tell you precisely what it tastes like: in a word, "sweet". And in two words, "*really* sweet". If cloying, pink cocktails are your thing then far be it from us to talk you out of one. After all, rocking up to Raffles does feel incredibly special, and drinking their Sling is surely a thing to tick off that bucket list. Your call.

Originally called the **Gin Sling,** it was invented prior to 1915 at the hotel's Long Bar by Hainanese bartender Ngiam Tong Boon. Over the years, the gin-based concoction has undergone a few tweaks but the current version is said to be close to the original. As per the International Bartenders Association info, the accepted recipe runs thus:
3 cl gin
1.5 cl cherry brandy
0.75 cl Cointreau
0.75 cl Benedictine
1 cl grenadine
12 cl pineapple juice
1.5 cl lime juice and a dash
    of bitters
Shaken over ice, the strained liquid (did we mention how pink it is?) is served in a highball glass, garnished with a wedge of pineapple and the inevitable maraschino cherry. Because that's how they rolled in the Edwardian era.

Martini Bar at The Grand Hyatt

Druggists

Dempsey Cookhouse Bar

The Rooftop's Negroni

THE SPIFFY DAPPER
2F/73 Amoy Street. 6pm-1am, daily

Amoy Street has loads of bars and this dark, moody one, up a ramshackle set of stairs, is surely one of the best. On purpose, it's easy to miss and by day it's a cool cafe. Come 6pm though and it takes on the allure of a 1920s speakeasy, complete with the appropriate music. They're known for cocktails and if you tell the barman what you're in the mood for, he'll concoct something from his vast repertoire to tick all your boxes.

DRUGGISTS
119 Tyrwhitt Road. 4pm-12am, daily

Occupying a 1931 Chinese drugstore, this fun, funky outlet is all about craft beers and food to go with them – think salted egg poutine fries, sliders and the like. It's in Singapore's hottest 'hood, popular with the hipster element for its mix of cafes, traditional eateries and cool bars. They've a 23-tap wall but come prepared to pony up for pints with a high ABV – they ain't cheap. Like, SGD30 not cheap, when the alcohol content lurches over the ridiculously high 15% mark.

THE DEMPSEY COOKHOUSE AND BAR
17D Dempsey Road. 12pm-3pm, 5pm-12am Mon-Fri, 12pm-1am Sat-Sun

This stylish, airy place has Jean-Georges Vongerichten stamped all over it – the legendary chef had input into not just the finessed food but the entire look and feel, including the bar, a large, U-shaped affair that soars architecturally upward towards the high ceiling. While the cucumber martini, mandarin mojito, ginger margarita and the like are great, it's really the calm, garden-like feel of the place, and the way it's bathed in ▷

BARS

sunlight during the day, that are the scene-stealers.

LANTERN BAR
5/F, The Fullerton Bay Hotel, 80 Collyer Quay. 8am-1am Sun-Thurs, 8am-2am Fri-Sat

This swish bar on the roof of The Fullerton Bay Hotel is a real CBD highlight. Especially when the sun is slinking low and there's a thunderstorm brewing; the views are stupendous. Pair your Caribbean-inspired cocktail with a round of wagyu beef sliders and kick back – the feel is breezy and unpretentious. They might have a Latin band playing and there's even a pool to dip in, if you came prepared.

MARTINI BAR, GRAND HYATT SINGAPORE (see pg 109)
10 Scotts Road. 4am-12am Mon-Tues, 4pm-1am Wed-Sat, 12am-12am Sun

This place is sexy! Wrapped in glass on the hotel's mezzanine level, the slick bar offers more than 40 types of martini, including berry, botanical, passionfruit, lychee, grapefruit and cosmopolitan flavoured ones. Every night, from 6pm until 9pm, they run a half-price offer on selected martinis, muddles, bubbles and house wines.

THE ROOFTOP, POTATO HEAD FOLK
36 Keong Saik Road. 5pm-late, daily

The wedge-shaped low-rise art deco building is a classic and inside, each level reveals a homey, intimate space that's either a bar or dining room. On the roof is a whimsical, tiki-themed, open-air bar, illuminated at night by strings of fairy lights. It's beautifully casual – slouch at the bar and chat to the friendly barman as he makes a text-book Aperol spritz, martini or hibiscus-infused margarita.

Lantern Bar

The bar at The Spiffy Dapper

Martini Bar

Smoke & Mirrors

A quiet corner at Raffles

Aperol spritz at The Rooftop

LOOF
331 North Bridge Road. 5pm-1am Mon-Thurs, 5pm-2am Fri-Sat

One of Singapore's hottest rooftop bars, this one brims with quirky, nostalgic vibes. The large open-air area is nestled in greenery and offers views over the CBD. Drinks are Asian-inspired and so is the terrific snacking menu – no one ever regretted chilli crab cheese fries, after all. Even better, you can play Beer Pong, a popular drinking game, shop for nostalgic tidbits at their little shop AND enjoy a sliding scale happy hour (drinks are $5 from5pm-5.59pm, $6 from 6pm-6.69pm, and $7 from 7pm-7.59pm).

BITTERS AND LOVE
118 Telok Ayer Street. 6pm-12am (closed Sun)

Cool. Very. The cocktail list runs to six 'all-time favourites' and after that, it's up to you and the barmen. They'll consult with you to figure your preferences and craft a drink from there. The space is intimate, with semi-industrial flourishes (rendered walls, tiled floors) but it's cosy too, seating just 60. Line your stomach with their smart bar food – oysters, burger or *flammekuchen*, for example.

NUTMEG & CLOVE
10A Ann Siang Hill. 6pm-1am Mon-Thurs, 6pm-2am Fri

It's Bar Central around here, with ever so many options. This one makes a feature of Singapore's history by taking a collection of William Farquhar's natural history drawings as a starting point for the cocktail menu. It's carved up among Herb, Spice, Fruits and Flora flavours, giving rise to concoctions like the King & Queen, a dramatic mix of durian, mangosteen, coffee, pandan, lemon, milk and overproof rum. ◆

CHILLI AND GINGER
CLAYPOT FROG WITH
CONGEE ON THE SIDE

Frog. Porridge. And look. We get that this dish might not be high on your culinary hit list but there are reasons why it's so popular. Good, delicious and healthy ones, even. Granted, bulge-eyed, bumpy-skinned amphibians aren't pretty critters but they sure taste good, given half a chance.

FROG PORRIDGE

If it helps, think of frogs as 'field chickens', a Chinese nickname for them. Frog meat contains less fat than chicken breast for similar amounts of protein, and they yield goodies like vitamins A, B6, B12, D, E and some K. Plus a slew of minerals too, potassium, iron, zinc, copper and selenium among them. The Chinese believe frog meat can cure male impotence (thumbs up!), can prevent asthma and cancer (double thumbs up!) and is said to be beneficial for diabetics (yay!). Chinese medicine also determines that frog meat has antibiotic properties (impressive) and can help wounds heal quickly, which is handy to know.

The Chinese have long revered frog meat – at one stage it was reserved for the Emperor's exclusive consumption. There's a frog-derived delicacy called *hashima*, which you can find locally; it's the dried fallopian tubes of lady frogs (true story) and is used, rehydrated, in local desserts with ▷

FROG PORRIDGE

names like 'snow jelly'. That's the frog bit explained; all you need to know about the porridge part here is that it's stand-your-spoon-up thick and made with rice. Gentle, soothing and delicious congee, no less.

Live frogs, ready to go...

In Singapore, there are two different styles of the dish. The first is simple and relatively unembellished – the fresh frog meat is cooked directly in the congee, a bit of ground pepper and some chopped coriander or green onion go over the top and that's it. The second version is where the frog is cooked separately in a thick soy-based sauce, amped up with chilli, ginger and garlic. It's often served separate to the congee or ladled on top and you aren't meant to stir the saucy frog bits into the congee. The aim is to scoop porridge and saucy frog in such a way to allow for fully savouring the different flavours and textures.

A portion of frog porridge

A few notes on the frogs – they're the badass American bullfrog (they'll eat their own for breakfast, if that's the only option) and they're locally farmed for the table. Growing about 15cm long, the National University of Singapore reported in 2009 that around 15 million frogs are consumed each year in Singapore – that's about five million kilos of meat. There's a concentration of frog porridge restaurants in Geylang, and the dish is eaten in the evening. It's expensive, relatively, because the frogs take time to mature and most of the meat is in the legs – which aren't large. ◆

Green onion garnish

WHERE TO EAT

EMINENT FROG PORRIDGE
323 Geylang Road, Lorong 19.
5pm-4am, daily
An institution, this place runs 'buy two get one free' frog deals. Order the *kungpo* frog, with its spicy, full-flavoured sauciness and lashings of green onion. They do plenty of other frog, and frog-free, dishes as well.

LION CITY FROG PORRIDGE
235 Geylang Road, Lorong 9.
3pm-3.30am, daily
Also called Shi Cheng, so don't be confused! A stall inside a coffee shop, it's a solid choice on the Geylang Road strip, although, as is common along here, there's no aircon. The signature is *kungpo* frog, where the super succulent meat and the punchy-sweet sauce are The Business, especially with their gutsy congee. The frog with ginger and spring onion is also a winner.

G7 SINMA CLAYPOT LIVE SEAFOOD
161-163 Geylang Road, Lorong 3.
3pm-3.30am, daily
As the name suggests, this *zi char* (Chinese home cooking) place serves more than frog; there's plenty of seafood, chicken, beef and beancurd dishes

FROG PORRIDGE
too. But you're here for the frog, right? As well as with porridge, have them deep fried with bean paste or ginger, or cooked with white pepper, ginger and green onion. They have lots of deals – buy four frogs and get three more free, for example.

TIONG SHIAN PORRIDGE CENTRE
265 New Bridge Road.
8am-4am, daily
A simple coffee shop in Chinatown, the location, long hours and large portions make it a handy choice. It's cheaper than most other frog places, and the menu takes you to plenty of places other than frog too. They have an extensive list of porridges (like cuttlefish) and sides, such as raw fish and braised beancurd. Note that you order with the cashier, not at your table.

A-ONE CLAYPOT HOUSE
#B2-25 Vivo City 1 Harbourfront Walk.
10am-10pm, daily
Those traditional claypots maintain optimal heat and eliminate the need to cook with loads of oil. The emphasis at this modern place is on health (no MSG), absolute freshness and good, old-fashioned flavour. It's airconned as well as being contemporary in feel; the claypot chilli frog is terrific. It's a chain so there are a number of outlets around.

129

Singapore does many things well. Neatness.
Greenness. Zoos. High Net Worth Individuals.
Saying 'lah'. Crab. Shopping As National Pastime.
Yes, the retail here is bonkers and resistance to its
lure, futile. So spend *lah*. Now *lah*. Here's where *lah*.

MELAMINE PLATES

Hawker centres and budget restaurants Asia-wide favour melamine – that
hard, smooth plastic that sort of resembles ceramic but, unlike crockery,
won't smash when dropped. Light and durable, it's fashioned into everything
from bowls, plates, cups and saucers to chopsticks. The clever cookies at The
Little Dröm Store, a design company founded by two graphic artists, make a
range of melamine plates emblazoned with illustrations of iconic Singapore
dishes. Find them at **The Farm Store**.
261 Waterloo Street. #04-20, 1pm-6pm Mon-Fri

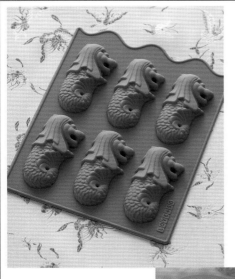

ICE TRAY

Witty little collectables that milk Singapore's beloved national icons for all they're worth, and then some – Love SG make clever things. Such as this merlion-shaped ice tray – because there's nothing that tops a bunch of merlions clanging in your cocktail. Just don't hurl like one afterwards. Find these, and other Love SG's wares, at one of design store **Naiise**'s six outlets.
**277 Orchard Road
Orchard Gateway,
#02-24.
11am-10pm, daily**

PINEAPPLE TARTS

They're associated with Lunar New Year but you can get a tart at any time these days. A good one should have a chewy, sticky glob of jam on a buttery, sweet-salty hand-crimped pastry base – although there are other shapes too. Such as the stuffed lozenges here. Most cake shops and confectioners sell them packaged to go – we like the hand-made ones from Katong's **Kim Choo Kueh Chang**.
**111 East Coast Road.
10am-10pm, daily**

BOOKS

Singapore's main **Kinokuniya** bookstore is nirvana for book lovers; prepare to spend time and $ here. Look for gems from local publishers such as these adorable titles by Epigram, a series focusing on Hokkien, South Indian, Peranakan, Eurasian, Cantonese or Teochew cuisine. Each volume delivers around 90 authentic recipes. **#04-21 Takashimaya Shopping Centre, 391 Orchard Road. 10am-9.30pm Sun-Fri, 10am-10pm Sat**

CERAMICS

Ng Seok Har and Michelle Lim work out of a studio near Little India, creating hand-thrown bowls, plates, cups, teapots and mugs etc. Called **Mud Rock Ceramics**, all the clay and glazes are mixed from scratch for their signature items, which have a functional, earthy beauty. Their pieces are in demand by top restaurants and the pair also run workshops, if you're keen to learn the craft. **85 Maude Rd, Rochor. Hours by appointment: email mudrockceramics@ gmail.com**

FRIDGE MAGNETS

Seasoned travellers know that populating a fridge door with the right souvenir magnets, those small but vital reminders of every trip taken, requires serious thought. The magnet must be strong, the materials should be unbreakable and the overall design, clever. No one wants naffness on their white goods. Once again, the team from The Little Dröm Store tick every box. Find their fun range at either **Naiise** (see pg 131) or **The Farm Store** (see pg 130).

SCENTED CANDLE

Yeah, yeah, we hate a scented candle on the dining table too. Just don't. Use this luxury one to freshen your bathroom when guests come to dine. It's from perfumer **Sifr Aromatics**, who make soy wax candles plus gorgeous fragrances, including bespoke scents. Johari Kazura is the charming owner and it was his grandfather who started the business in 1933.
42 Arab St, Kampong Glam. 11am-8pm, Mon-Sat, 11am-5pm Sun

VINEGAR & SOY

Asian epicures! **COMO Marketplace** is your new Happy Place; it's packed with artisanal ingredients. There are premium Chinese sausages from Canada, Sarawak peppercorns from Malaysia and this Thai coconut vinegar, for starters. Look for Kwong Woh Hing soy sauces, a lauded, naturally brewed soy from Singapore. And excellent spice pastes and sambals by local brand Batu Lesung.
**Block 17B,
Dempsey Road.
11.30am-9pm, daily**

CHOCOLATE

Cat Socrates is a beloved neighbourhood bookstore but they stock other stuff too. Such as chocolate from local boutique producer Fossa – expect tropically-inspired flavours like lychee-rose, chilli-peanut praline, candied ginger and salted egg cereal. They do everything from scratch, including cracking, roasting, and winnowing cocoa beans before fashioning the chocolate.
**448 Joo Chiat Road,
Katong.
12.30pm-9.30pm
(closed Mon)**

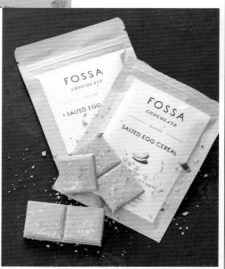

PAPER WEIGHTS

Another goodie from **The Farm Store** (see pg 130). A bit hard to find (it's not far from the Bugis MRT), it's more showroom than shop. You purchase online (they'll let you use their wifi) as they don't physically process cash or card sales, but their range of locally designed, Singapore-themed wares is stupendous. You could totally make this a one-stop shopping destination. Case in point are these adorable ceramic paper weights, perfectly shaped like moon cakes, complete with typical pastry detailing.

SOCKS

Because nothing stimulates wonderful food memories like staring at your ankles, these fun socks from **When I Was Four** make a perfect foodie memento. Also available in satay, chicken rice, durian and *ang ku kueh* designs, they're 35% cotton/65% polyester and are unisex, up to men's UK size 10.5.

**#02-18,
261 Waterloo Street.
12pm-2pm, 3pm-
7.30pm Tues-Fri,
12.30pm-6.30pm Sat,
12.30pm-5.30pm Sun**

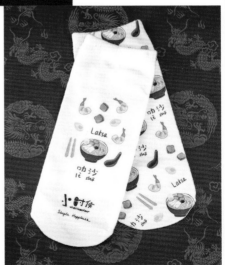

Notes

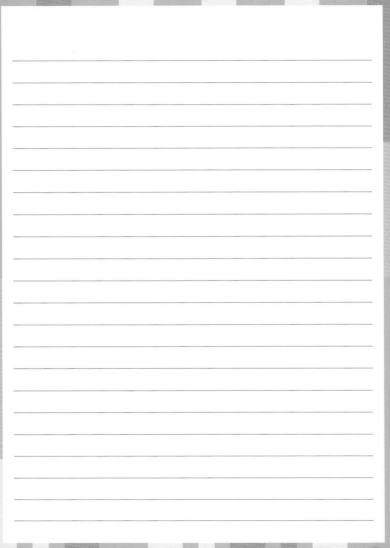

Singapore In 12 Dishes
Published by RedPorkPress
P.O. Box 10003, Dominion Road, Auckland, 1446 New Zealand
www.redporkpress.com

 www.facebook.com/redporkpress
 www.instagram.com/redporkpress
 www.twitter.com/redporkpress

Publishing executive: Antony Suvalko
Editorial director: Leanne Kitchen
Art direction and design: Anne Barton
Copy editor: Judy Pascoe
Words and photography: ©RedPorkPress

©2019 RedPorkPress

RedPorkPress would like to thank **The Singapore Tourism Board, Hotel Indigo Singapore Katong** and **The Fullerton Hotel Singapore** for their kind assistance in the making of this book.

First edition – January 2019

ISBN 9780473443337

Printed in China

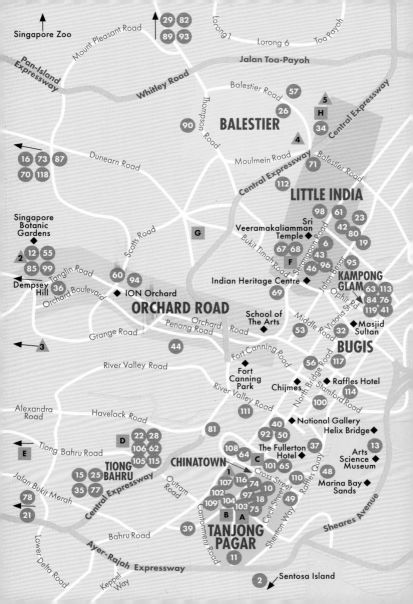